Chronology of Transportation
in the United States

Chronology of Transportation in the United States

RUSSELL O. WRIGHT

McFarland & Company, Inc., Publishers
Jefferson, North Carolina, and London

LIBRARY OF CONGRESS CATALOGUING-IN-PUBLICATION DATA

Wright, Russell O.
    Chronology of transportation in the United States /
Russell O. Wright.
      p.   cm.
    Includes bibliographical references (p.) and index.

    ISBN 0-7864-1791-9 (softcover : 50# alkaline paper) ∞

    1. Transportation — United States — History — Chronology.
I. Title.
HE203.W75   2004
388'.0973 — dc22   2004004458

British Library cataloguing data are available

Cover photograph ©2004 Corbis Images

Manufactured in the United States of America

*McFarland & Company, Inc., Publishers
  Box 611, Jefferson, North Carolina 28640
  www.mcfarlandpub.com*

To Halina

ACKNOWLEDGMENTS

I want to acknowledge the help of my wife, Halina, and my daughter, Terry Ann Wright, in completing this book. Halina acquired research material from the *Los Angeles Times*, the Internet, and our local library. She also served as an editor who was a nitpicker in the best possible way.

Terry, as she has on my previous books in this series, typed much of the final manuscript, created the figures shown in the appendices, and arranged the manuscript when it was finished. She surfed the Internet as needed, ordering research books and acquiring research material from an endless variety of sources. She also arranged the voluminous files in my den, keeping a sense of order so that I could focus my time on the process of researching and writing the book.

Many authors are able to say that they were helped by the encouragement of their families, but it is one thing to have family members stand by on the sidelines and shout encouragement and quite another to have family members actually take an active part in the work. When they do, continual progress can be made on the book every day.

I also want to acknowledge the contributions of the authors of the books listed in the bibliography. Whatever the subject, the authors who have gone before, uncovering facts and compiling data, often plowing unfurrowed ground, always make the job easier for those of us who follow.

CONTENTS

INTRODUCTION

This chronology covers four centuries' development of commercial and private transportation in America, beginning with the arrival of the first Pilgrims, around 1600. For most of the two hundred years between 1600 and 1800, the main means of transportation, other than by foot, was by horse-drawn wagon or carriage, primarily imported from Europe. Although the wheel was invented around 3500 B.C. in the Middle East, and was probably developed independently in Europe around 1400 B.C., it was never independently invented in the New World. The wheel was unknown to the great Inca, Aztec, and Mayan civilizations, and the Indian tribes of the plains in the United States were still dragging their goods on poles pulled by their horses (called a "travois") when they saw their first "white men."

The horses had been evolving for tens of millions of years, starting on what are now the Great Plains of the United States. They emigrated across ancient land bridges to Asia, and then developed in the East. Curiously, an earlier strain in the East had gone extinct, and the Great Plains horses also became extinct after some had emigrated to Asia. Thus, horses were reintroduced to the West by the Spanish Conquistadors, among others, and were here when the Pilgrims arrived, although many more were brought from Europe.

As a result, the initial means of transportation in the colonies were on foot, on horseback, or in wagons and carriages pulled by horses (or oxen or mules). Water transportation was possible using nearly anything that floated and could be steered on the streams and rivers, which were not necessarily in the most convenient places. In a country as large as the United States, it took a long time to travel any substantial distance using these primitive means of transportation. For example, around 1800, a boat simply floating with the current took more than 40 days to reach New Orleans from Louisville, a city considered well to the west on the Ohio River. This is one of the reasons that Congress, fearful of creating such a large territory that it must eventually split into separate political units, approved President Jefferson's acquisition of the Louisiana Purchase in 1803 with many misgivings.

Although little changed in terms of transportation in the first 200 years after the Pilgrims began arriving, the next two centuries brought changes that no one could have imagined in the early 1800s. From a geographically fragmented fledgling nation, the United States grew into an economic colossus, the whole country one enormous market connected by road, air, rail, and even the airwaves. These changes were triggered by James Watt's development of the first practical steam engine, in 1769. In 1807 Robert Fulton's steamboat, the *Clermont* (using an English steam engine), was operating on the Hudson River. By 1811, Nicholas Roosevelt developed a river steamboat that could paddle its way from Pittsburgh, where the Ohio River begins, to New Orleans, in just 14 days compared to the more than 40 days it previously took for the shorter trip from Louisville to New Orleans. By 1819 Moses Rogers was setting out for England in the world's first oceangoing steamship. This was just a drop in the bucket compared to the changes brought about in the United States by the use of the steam engine for rail transportation.

However, before we leap ahead, we need to consider the painful progress, such as it was, that was made in the forms of transportation used in the United States prior to the great advances that came with the introduction of the steamship, the railroad, and the steam locomotive. The first roads in the United States were essentially trails made by deer and other animals, and these trails were further smoothed by generations of Indians. The arrival of Europeans in the New World added the use of the horse (and other hoofed animals) as well as carts and wagons to the transportation system, greatly increasing the distances that people could travel, although the network of existing trails could not always easily accommodate these new means of transportation.

There were two important transportation developments in the very early history of the United States. One took place along the eastern seaboard, and another in the thrust to the West. On the eastern seaboard, trails were turned into roads quickly enough that by 1700 it was possible for an individual to ride on horseback without interruption from Boston to Philadelphia, then the center of the colonial world. So-called stage wagons were developed in individual colonies soon after, and by 1771 a stage coach (dubbed the "flying machine") offered public transportation (in good weather) between New York and Philadelphia in only a day and a half, with overnight lodging provided as needed. In 1776 it took General Washington a full 12 days to get to his command in Boston, but the crude highway system on the seaboard permitted travel for wheeled vehicles from the future site of the United States Capital, in Maryland, all the way to the coastal city of Portsmouth, in New Hampshire.

In the move to the West, fur traders used the trails already established by the Indians. The cattlemen who followed searching for suitable pastures, made the trails a little wider and miners and lumbermen further widened the trails, although they made greater use of available waterways. Finally, the first farmers began to turn the trails into primitive roads so their packhorses could carry supplies and crops back and forth between their markets and their farms. Established farmers needed roads to carry carts in the summer and sleighs in the winter. The towns that grew up in the same regions demanded better roads for similar reasons. So, step-by-step, primitive roads were developed in the "wilderness" areas.

The period from 1750 to 1800 saw a continual improvement in these fundamental roadways, but local governments would not or could not levy the taxes needed to improve or expand the roads. As a result, entrepreneurs stepped in and started the toll road movement, in which the collection of tolls would pay for construction and maintenance of the roads over time. A charter was granted to the Philadelphia and Lancaster (Pennsylvania) Turnpike Company in 1792, marking the start of a new era. Lancaster was about 62 miles due west of Philadelphia, and the turnpike was constructed in less than two years. The highway was 37 feet wide, and was paved with stone covered with gravel. It was an immediate success, and was crowded with a mixture of attractive private chaises, stagecoaches, farm carts and wagons, large emigrant wagons on their way west, and individuals on horseback.

As the Philadelphia-Lancaster turnpike began to pay large dividends, it was quickly extended about 20 miles to the Susquehanna River, and it began to be widely copied. The Catskill Turnpike was built between New York City and the Catskill Mountains by 1804, and it was soon followed by the Mohawk and Hudson Turnpike running west from Albany. Turnpike fever spread nearly everywhere. By 1821, Pennsylvania had chartered 146 turnpike companies and Massachusetts had chartered nearly the same number. New York had over 4,000 miles of turnpike roads, and Baltimore had become the third largest city in the United States thanks in part to her seven trunk-line turnpikes.

Virginia built its famous Shenandoah Valley turnpike, a heavily used road that was 92 miles long. It was so well built that about 40 years later, in the Civil War, five Baltimore and Ohio locomotives seized by the South were rolled down the highway to a Southern depot without denting the surface of the roadway. South Carolina built a turnpike between Charleston and Columbia, and the so-called National Road, intended to run 700 miles from Maryland to Illinois (then considered part of the western frontier), started to carry traffic in August of 1817. Individuals and companies alike learned the value of quick and reliable transportation throughout the states that had turnpikes.

In the meantime, manufacturers of wheeled vehicles were developing the buckboard, the spring-wagon, the so-called buggy, and various farm work-wagons. For heavier loads they developed the Concord coach (an elegant and comfortable wagon intended mainly for passenger travel), and the famous Conestoga wagon for hauling freight. There were many other types copied or adapted from vehicles in use in Europe, but the Americans were rapidly developing a vehicle-manufacturing capability of their own. The Concord, invented by a builder in New Hampshire around 1825, was widely copied, and specific models were still being used for local transportation in the West in the 1880s.

The Conestoga wagon was the freight car of those pre-railroad days, and it made its appearance about 50 years before the Revolutionary War. It was developed in the Conestoga River Valley near Lancaster, Pennsylvania. Thousands were built to support the movement of freight during the war and after. The bottom of the wagon had a characteristic dish shape to help prevent loads from shifting during travel up and down hills. They were widely used in the southeastern Pennsylvania area where they were developed and the neighboring areas of Maryland and beyond. The Conestoga wagon proved so useful and popular that it evolved into the best method for getting freight over the Allegheny Mountains of Pennsylvania and into the "western" regions of Ohio and Indiana. With the standard six horses (or oxen or mules) pulling it, the ensemble was 60 feet long with the white canvas cover reaching 11 feet high. The rear wheels were five to six feet in diameter. When not walking by the side, the driver occupied a small seat on the left side of the wagon and this, according to legend, led to the habit of American drivers' keeping to the right side of the road. Professional drivers of the Conestoga often smoked a long, thin, cheap cigar, available at four for a penny, which led to that kind of cigar being called a "stogie."

Contrary to popular belief, the Conestoga wagon was not the wagon normally used to take settlers and their families on their way to settle west of the Mississippi River. The original Conestoga wagons were far too heavy for the task. A descendant of the Conestoga wagon, called the prairie schooner because its characteristic white canvas top made it look like the old ocean-going schooners when the wagon made its way across the high grass of the prairies, carried most settlers west. The schooner was much lighter than the Conestoga wagon, and whereas the wagon required six horses to pull it, the lighter schooner could make do with four or even two horses. Many times oxen were used in place of horses. The schooner was actually little more than a big farm wagon with its top providing cover for the women and children who slept and usually rode inside. These vehicles made up the famous wagon

trains of the West, traveling together for reasons of safety, although some Conestoga wagons went west on freight-carrying voyages and also traveled in
wagon trains.

In the course of practicing their trade, various carriage and wagon manufacturers made many technological advancements. Choices of wood for the
various parts; suitable springs for comfort and durability; oil-lubricated axles
that would turn easily for a long time; and the various pieces of hardware,
such as door hinges, all required years of experimentation to perfect the designs.
This developed not only an industry of carriage makers, but also a long list
of specialists to supply parts to the industry. This thriving industry was thus
ready to supply the methods of transportation that would follow — the railroad and the automobile. The Studebaker brothers, among the most successful builders of wagons (they advertised themselves as "wagon makers and
blacksmiths"), would go on to play a role in the automobile business. As
often happens, they were not as successful after becoming car manufacturers as they had been when manufacturing car parts.

The Advent of Steam Locomotives and the Railroad

Brief mention should be made of the invention of the steam engine by
James Watt in 1769 and its utilization in steamboats in the United States,
starting with Robert Fulton's *Clermont* in 1807. About the same time, beginning in the 1780s, canals were being built in the United States to allow water
transportation where natural waterways did not exist.

Perhaps the most famous was New York State's Erie Canal, which was
opened in 1825. This created a waterway that was an easy route to the Great
Lakes region and what was then the western frontier. It was immensely successful, and many other (usually shorter) canals were built in the United States.
But the same year the Erie Canal was built, John Stevens, of Hoboken, New
Jersey, built the first experimental steam locomotive in the United States.
Thus, the year the Erie Canal opened, the very thing that would render it
obsolete, the railroad, was being born. The railroad would eclipse all other
existing methods of transportation, and the development of the railroads across
the country would be the biggest business in the United States for the rest
of the nineteenth century.

The idea of a steam locomotive that would run on a track quickly followed the 1769 development of the steam engine by Watt. By 1802 an experimental locomotive was running in Wales, and in 1829 John Stephenson and
his father, George, produced a locomotive called "The Rocket." It had a top
speed of 36 mph and was the first man-made land vehicle that could outrun
a horse. The concept was quickly copied in the United States, and in 1829

Peter Cooper built the first passenger locomotive in the country, the famous Tom Thumb, built for the Baltimore and Ohio Railroad. When it was placed into service, it started a railroad boom in the United States. Railroads were far cheaper to build than canals (and even good roads for that matter), and they could haul huge loads of bulky freight at very low costs. It was said in California after the transcontinental railroad was completed in 1869 that it cost more for a farmer to move his grain ten miles over the inadequate roads to the train depot than it cost to get the grain shipped to New York.

Thirty years later, in 1860, the United States had built over 31,000 miles of railroad, more than one thousand miles per year, even though most of it was east of the Mississippi River. Such a building program was reasonable in a country of great distances that had plenty of coal (more than any other country) to fire the locomotives and large forests from which to make railroad ties and bridges. An infant steel manufacturing industry (based on the vast coal resources) was growing ever larger to produce steel rails. Pressure was building to extend the railroads to California, which at that time could be reached only by a very dangerous overland trip by horse and wagon, or by long sea voyages around South America or to the Isthmus of Panama, with a dangerous overland voyage across the isthmus. There was also fear that California and the other coastal states would follow the lead of the Confederacy, and leave the Union. A transcontinental railroad would help to tie the western states to the Union. Finally, President Abraham Lincoln had spent most of his career as a lawyer acting on behalf of the railroads. He was an expert in railroad affairs, and he was determined to see a transcontinental railway built.

Actually, a transcontinental railroad had been discussed in the United States for nearly three decades, ever since the first train began running. The population had grown from 12.8 million in 1830 to 31 million in 1860, passing Great Britain when it hit 23 million in 1850. Railroads were the preferred method of transportation for all those millions, and the state of Pennsylvania alone, blessed with huge deposits of both coal and iron, had more rail manufacturers than all of England. The biggest obstacle to getting a coast-to-coast railway built was a very common one — politics.

When Congress called for a survey in 1853 to determine the best way west, Jefferson Davis, then secretary of war, sent four teams out to complete the task. Four routes were proposed, from near the Mexican and Canadian borders, and along the 49th and 32nd parallels. The area west of the Mississippi had been thought of as the "Great American Desert," but the reports indicated that much of the area had excellent agricultural prospects and was suitable for settlement. There were also areas with fine mineral prospects (gold had been discovered in California in 1848, but Nevada and other states had good deposits of silver and other minerals). The surveyors had done an outstanding job, and eventually railroads would be built along all four proposed routes. But not the first transcontinental railroad.

The issue of slavery stopped any action in Congress. Davis and fellow southerners wanted a southern route, but "Free Soilers" wanted a northern route so that slavery would not be extended westward. Neither side would budge. The election of Lincoln as president in 1860 ironically resolved the issue. In April of 1861, about one month after Lincoln's inauguration, the Confederate states fired on Fort Sumter, and the Civil War was underway. The Confederate states were no longer in Congress, and it was now possible to pass a bill to build the transcontinental railroad.

Lincoln, ever a railroad buff, had even taken a turn at driving the locomotive on the train that had taken him from Springfield, Illinois, to Washington to begin his presidency. He was much more concerned with holding the country together than having a railroad built, but now it was possible to work on both tasks. He authorized a line to be built along the 42nd parallel up the Platte River Valley. It would link up with a line being built eastward from Sacramento, California, through the Sierra Nevada mountain range and on into Nevada and Utah. The Union Pacific Company would be created to build the line westward while the Central Pacific railroad, already established in California, would build the line eastward.

The transcontinental railroad was to be paid for by land grants from the United States government. They had plenty of land to exchange for the railroad, and since they maintained land along the route as they gave it away in alternate chunks to the railroad builders, much of the land they kept greatly increased in value as the railroad was built. On paper — and, as it turned out, in fact — it was a win-win situation. There were the usual financial scandals involved with such a project, and individuals (including members of Congress) enriched themselves at the public trough while essentially bankrupting the Union Pacific company (although it continued to operate and eventually prospered). The owners of the Central Pacific railroad in California, Charles Crocker, Collis Huntington, Leland Stanford, and Mark Hopkins, became synonymous with avarice and greed — and great riches and power after the railroad was built. But they did in fact build it, often putting their own money at risk as they went along. The person who got it started, Theodore Judah, had a falling out with the other four men, who later bought out his share. He died of yellow fever before construction was well under way. He never saw his dream completed, and he was largely forgotten after the transcontinental railroad was finished.

Congress wrote the bills authorizing the transcontinental railroad in a way that encouraged the two sides to engage in a race to see how far they could get before linking up, which was a strong incentive for the use of subterfuge on both sides. The line was built much faster than anyone imagined it would be. The initial legislation authorizing the line was passed by Congress in 1862, and anticipated a finish date of 1876. The bill was horrendously complex and would have to be re-written and clarified in the future, but the game was on. The line was officially begun in 1863 and completed by the middle of 1869, well in advance of the deadline. An excellent account of the building of the transcontinental railroad can be found in the book *Nothing Like It in the World,* by historian Stephen E. Ambrose. Much of the following summary of the benefits that resulted from the railroad were drawn from this book.

A corollary benefit of funding the transcontinental railroad (and other railroads in the United States during the 1800s) was that Wall Street financiers, good and bad, learned how to sell the stocks and bonds associated with building railroads. One could say that with all of its other economic benefits, the advent of the railroad also brought Wall Street, as we know it now, through its adolescence. Railroads created a major economic boom in the United States in the 1800s, and became themselves the major employer in the country. Though they were just a part of the total impact of railroads, the benefits of the transcontinental railroad alone make a very impressive list.

During the California gold rush, starting in 1848, before the rail line was complete, getting from New York to San Francisco took several months, whether by sea around South America, by horse and wagon from the Mississippi, or a combined sea and land journey via the Isthmus of Panama. It could cost more than $1,000 to make the trip, a considerable sum in those days. One week after the line was complete, the trip was reduced to seven days, with first-class costing $150, and "emigrant" class costing $70. In a year, first-class Pullman sleeping cars were down to $136, and sitting on a bench in emigrant class was $65.

Freight rates on trains were similarly cheaper than wagons, sailboats, or steamers. Mail that previously cost dollars per ounce and was extremely slow now cost pennies and moved from Chicago to California in a few days. The telegraph, invented in 1844, had stretched across the country in 1861 and was a key aid in building the railroad. The railroad was required by law to include a telegraph line as it went across the nation, and local train stations included the local telegraph office as well. Communication from Europe or England to New York to California or any telegraph station in between was almost instantaneous. The completion of the railroad meant there were more than forty thousand miles of track in the Unites States, 40 percent of all the track in the world. In late 1868 one magazine said that, because of the railroads, production in the United States had increased by 230 percent, while the population had increased by only 90 percent.

There were many special problems in the transcontinental project because the emphasis was primarily on finishing quickly. The American people were fascinated by the contest between the two sides, and railroads in general at that time operated on the premise that the rails should be laid as quickly as possible so that revenues could be collected as soon as possible. Problems could then be fixed with profits derived from operating the railroad rather than the borrowing of more money. Near the end of the transcontinental project, in the drive to get more mileage and thus more money, the two sides were furiously grading in opposite directions in full sight of each other. The Central Pacific did a better job of playing politics than the Union Pacific, so although the official meeting place was Promontory Point (Promontory Summit), the Central Pacific owned the right-of-way to Ogden, Utah, about 50 miles farther east. The Union Pacific had to sell those 50 miles of track to the Central Pacific soon after the ceremony was held with the famous golden spike at Promontory Summit.

The biggest project of the 19th century was followed quickly by the biggest scandal of the century. In September of 1872, the *New York Times* featured a headline that started "The King of Frauds" in bold capitals at the top of the page. The headline went on to attack the Credit Mobilier, the company established by the Union Pacific to build the line — a company whose stock created fortunes for many men, including members of Congress. There were, of course, positive arguments to be made about the land grant technique and the use of government-guaranteed bonds and loans to build a project as massive and as useful to the whole country as the transcontinental railroad. The government eventually made an appropriate profit on its bonds and loans, and in addition the value of the land they held back from the project was greatly increased by the railroad's construction. The benefits of this government intervention are still being debated today, but at the time they were overwhelmed by the flavor of scandal. The Populist Party and later the Progressive Party were direct outgrowths of the scandal that followed the completion of the transcontinental railroad.

It could be said that in the 30 years between the completion of the transcontinental railroad and the end of the century, the railroad companies were too successful for their own good. They had what amounted to an absolute monopoly, and in too many instances they charged what the traffic would bear for their services. Farmers, with no competitive way to get their goods to the market, were especially incensed. The railroads suffered a grievous public relations blow when William H. Vanderbilt, son of the famous Cornelius "Commodore" Vanderbilt, and inheritor of the Vanderbilt fortune — including the New York Central Railroad — got into a fare fight with the Pennsylvania Railroad for passengers going to Chicago. Taken somewhat out of context, in an interview with the *Chicago Daily News* about the fare war, Vanderbilt was quoted as saying "The public be damned!"

The quote was given wide circulation, and it was taken to represent the arrogant attitude of the railroads in the 1880s. The Grange Movement, a self-help organization of farmers that had grown to over 800,000 members, was fired up by Vanderbilt's statement and redoubled its efforts to bring political pressure to achieve some control over railroad rates. One result was the formation of the Interstate Commerce Commission in 1887. At first the commission was ineffective, but by the beginning of the 1900s, the railroad companies realized that government regulation could quickly determine whether or not they survived. Nearly everyone outside the industry hated the railroads and was anxious to see them brought under control. This attitude and subsequent government regulation, plus competition from the new automotive and airline industries, practically destroyed the power of railroad companies by the end of the 1900s.

But as the 1800s drew to a close, railroads dominated nearly every aspect of public life. Only agriculture had more workers. In 1916, there were 1.7 million people working for the railroads, about four percent of the entire population of the country, and that did not include people working in industries like locomotive manufacturing that supplied the railroads. The miles of railway operated by the railroads peaked at 254,036 in 1916, and railroad wealth was about 15 percent of the total wealth of the United States in 1900. But by 2000, the track mileage was less than 132,000 miles, a drop of 36 percent since 1970, and less than it had been in 1886. At the end of the 1900s, railroads were nearly an anachronism, and certainly not considered big business. The fall of the railroads in the 20th century was almost as dramatic as their rise in the 19th century.

The Advent of the Bicycle in the 1890s

The 1890s were a period in which the bicycle represented a transition from the railroads to automotive and aircraft transportation. Bicycles made their first impact in the United States in the mid–1870s when a Boston retailer named Albert A. Pope introduced the "ordinary" bicycle (the bicycle with a very high wheel in front), which was somewhat tricky to ride. He copied the bike from an English model, and in 1878 contracted with the Weed Sewing Machine Company of Hartford to make an American version. He sold about a quarter-million high-wheeled bikes in the next decade.

Pope introduced the "safety" bike in 1887. The safety bike had two wheels of equal size and was much like the bikes of today. It was also copied from England, and it was much easier (and safer) to ride than the high-wheeled ordinary bike. The safety bike was an immediate success. A biking boom took place in the 1890s, and at its peak, over 300 companies were making the new bicycle, and more than one million per year were being produced.

One outgrowth of the bicycle craze was a demand for better roads upon which the bicycles could travel. This demand also was being made by early automobile clubs, and the government began an "object lesson" program to encourage local governments to budget money to pay for better roads. In 1897, an object lesson road was built at the New Jersey Agricultural College. It was on the main road to the college and was only 660 feet long, but it featured an eight-foot width of macadam to demonstrate how nice a new road could be for bicycles and cars. The road cost the government only $321— the first of many billions of dollars it would spend on roads in the next century. The cost was so low because Pope and his allies got the railroads and road equipment manufacturers to provide free equipment, and local government and individuals to contribute towards labor and materials. It is ironic that the railroads were of great help in getting the object lesson roads built and in supporting the "Good Roads" movement that followed. The railroads saw the Good Roads movement as a way of expanding their customer base beyond the three to ten mile radius around the depots that marked the end of paved roads in most locations. The railroads eventually realized that government payments for better roads amounted to a free subsidy for truckers, their competition. They finally stopped supporting the Good Roads movement, but by then it was too late for them.

Another effect of the bicycle craze was the number of suppliers who established themselves to support bicycle manufacturing. Many of them later became suppliers to the infant automobile industry. Others turned their attention to other areas. In Dayton, Ohio, a pair of brothers named Orville and Wilbur Wright, previously in the printing business, became fond of bike riding and decided to open a bicycle shop at the end of 1892. Most bike companies of the time relied upon the newly developed concepts of mass production, but the Wright brothers were like the old artisans, carefully crafting the bicycles one at a time. They were quite successful in spite of much competition, and by late 1896 others could run the business under the nominal direction of the two brothers. The brothers began casting about for new horizons to conquer, and manned flight was the next field they entered. Their bicycle manufacturing experience was very helpful in that venture.

The bicycle craze of the 1890s led directly to a national demand for better roads, and indirectly to the creation of the airplane by the Wright brothers. The demand for better roads helped to support what became a national craze for the cars of Henry Ford in the first decade of the next century, a period during which the Wright brothers, almost in anonymity compared to Henry Ford, showed the world that manned flight was possible. This first decade of the 20th century was the beginning of a new phase in transportation, and the beginning of the end of the power held by the still-arrogant railroads.

The Arrival of the Airplane and the Automobile

The arrival of the airplane and the automobile were probably the two most important events in the history of transportation, and in a practical sense they both arrived in the same year: 1908. That was the year that the Wright brothers first fully demonstrated their famous Flyer in France for the French military, and in the United States for the U.S. military at Fort Myer, Virginia. The same year Henry Ford first offered his famous Model T car for sale, and over 10,000 were sold in its first model year. Both industries had been in development for some time prior to 1908, especially the automobile industry, but both industries essentially entered the public consciousness of the United States — and the world — in 1908.

The Wright brothers were looking for a new endeavor in late 1896 as their bicycle business became well established and required less of their personal time. The death of Otto Lilienthal in August of 1896 caught their full attention. Lilienthal was famous, at least within the then tiny aeronautical world, and was known as "The Flying Man" for his over 2,000 leaps into the air while trying to fly gliders. His last flight, on August 9, 1896, ended in a crash that broke his spine, and he died the next day. This accident rekindled an interest in flight that the Wright brothers had developed from reading about Lilienthal's and other men's efforts.

The Wright brothers went about trying to build a flying machine in a very methodical way. They read the existing literature, contacted and started a friendship with a flight expert in his mid-60s, a civil engineer from Chicago named Oliver Canute who acted as a one-man clearing house for news about attempts at manned flight, and even did some kite-flying in Dayton in the summer of 1899. The crucial fact they recognized early was that one needed to learn how to control an aircraft in flight before attempting powered flight. Once a control system had been developed, adding a means of propulsion would be a relatively simple manner. They contacted the weather bureau to find out where the kinds of winds they needed for testing were most likely, and they concluded that Kitty Hawk, North Carolina, offered suitable winds at the right time of the year in a location that was not too far from Dayton. They built a glider and made their first trip to Kitty Hawk in September of 1900.

The Wright brothers made additional trips to Kitty Hawk in 1901 and 1902. They collected flight data on each trip, and they ran tests in their bicycle shop in Dayton aided by a homemade wind tunnel and other instruments. After their 1902 flight tests they were convinced that they knew how to achieve the necessary control in flight, and, with the encouragement of Oliver Canute, they began in early 1903 to build a motor and a propeller and to rebuild their glider to accept the additional weight (they called the new biplane the Flyer in anticipation of success). They were ready to attempt powered "heavier than air" flight when they went back to Kitty Hawk later in 1903.

On December 17, 1903, Wilbur Wright made the first powered flight. It was, as he said later, "the first flight in the history of the world in which a machine carrying a man had raised itself by its own power into the air in full flight, had sailed forward without reduction of speed, and had finally landed at a point as high as that from which it started." The brothers were able to make only a few more flights before the Flyer was too damaged in a crash landing for them to continue flying. Satisfied, they telegraphed news of their success back home, then packed up and headed for Dayton.

The brothers had planned a controlled release of the news, but it hardly made any public impact at all. Ironically, Samuel Langley, originally associated with the Smithsonian but working quietly with government support for several years, had tried to make a powered flight with his plane, the Aerodrome, being launched from a catapult on a houseboat anchored in the Potomac River in Washington. The plane appeared to have been damaged in the launching process, and it pointed straight up for a moment before falling into the river tail-first. Hordes of reporters had been on hand for several months, smelling a story in the poorly kept secrecy in which Langley was trying to work. There had been prior unsuccessful attempts, and by now the reporters were treating the whole process as a huge joke. The flight described above took place on December 8, 1903, only nine days before Wilbur Wright made his historic flight before a handful of spectators at Kitty Hawk.

The result was that some papers confused the news of the flight by the Wright brothers with that of Langley's disaster, and others put the brothers in the category of crackpots like Langley. The Wright brothers were not unhappy with the treatment. They had embarked on a series of strategic mistakes in public relations that were to hinder them for the rest of their time in the airplane business. They wanted to profit from their invention, but they went about it in just the wrong way, and they suffered the effects of hubris when they decided, incorrectly, that they were many years ahead of the many inventors around the world now trying to solve the problem of manned flight.

At first they tried to patent their method of flight control, and set out to do it themselves. The patent was delayed until 1906, after they finally hired a professional patent attorney to make their case. In the meantime they tried to keep the Flyer out of the public eye so that no one would steal their secrets. They continued their flight experiments in a field near Dayton, no longer needing the winds of Kitty Hawk to fly. During 1904 and 1905, the brothers made great improvements in Flyer II and Flyer III, and they themselves learned much more about how to pilot their airplane. But they also decided to undertake selling it themselves, and as has often been the case, the personalities of the people who invent new things are sometimes not well suited to the process of marketing their inventions. So it was with the Wright brothers. They essentially did nothing to improve their airplane for over two years while they played a "chicken and egg" game with various governments, refusing to make demonstration flights without first having a contract, while the governments refused to consider any contracts without demonstrations first. The brothers also did a poor job of separating themselves from nut cases clamoring for government support, rather than as possible contractors who already had built a viable airplane. They contented themselves with writing letters. If they had planned an in-person marketing campaign as methodically as they had planned the development of the plane, they might have succeeded much sooner in selling their invention. In the meantime, the rest of the world was catching up with them, something they thought was impossible given only a few years.

In 1908 the impasse was broken. The brothers had contracted to sell an airplane and pilot training to the United States Signal Corps, with demonstration flights to take place in Fort Myer, Virginia. They had also contracted to make demonstration flights in France as part of a process to have their aircraft built under license. They returned to Kitty Hawk in spring of 1908 to be sure they could handle the new Flyer's modified control system, which would permit a passenger to be carried (and to be sure of being left relatively alone while they experimented, as Kitty Hawk was not easy to get to). Wilbur then went to France to conduct demonstrations there, while Orville stayed behind to perform the demonstrations at Fort Myer. The results were absolutely sensational, and in a sense 1908 was the real beginning of the era of manned flight started by the Wright brothers, rather than 1903, when the first primitive attempt was completed.

Wilbur was first to amaze the world. He was flying a plane informally called the Flyer Model Λ, which was a modification of Flyer III from 1905. The brothers never officially used this designation, but they did call the next basic aircraft they built the Model B. At Le Mans, France, on Saturday, August 8, 1908, Wilbur launched into flight, climbed rapidly, casually banked into turns and circled round the field, landing after a flight of only a minute and 45 seconds. But the duration of the flight was not important. The obvious ease and command with which Wilbur flew the Flyer astonished the crowd. They were used to seeing planes hop and skip along the ground before getting into the air. Turns and banks were made slowly and with great care. Many in the crowd had come to scoff because the Wright brothers had operated in such secrecy that some people thought they might be frauds. The less than two minutes spent in the air by Wilbur made him a hero overnight.

A French pilot named Paul Zens, who had waited since morning to see the 6:30 pm flight, was quoted as saying, "I would have waited ten times as

long to have seen what I have seen today. Mr. Wright has us all in his hands."
In the same vein, another pilot, Rene Gasnier, said, "We are children compared to the Wrights." Renowned pilot Louis Bleriot, who in 1909 would
become the first person to fly over the English Channel, said, "a new era in
mechanic flight has commenced. I am not sufficiently calm after the event
to thoroughly express my opinion."

The following Monday Wilbur flew again, throwing in a figure eight
for good measure. The crowd went wild. Present that day was Leon Delagrange, one of the top pilots in France and a top figure in French aviation.
He had come down from Paris to see the show for himself because he couldn't
believe so much fuss was being made about such a brief flight. After watching Wilbur's flight, Delagrange was nearly overcome by emotion. His com-
ments appeared in the paper *Le Matin* the next morning: "Oh well. We are
beaten. We do not even exist."

While Wilbur was winning plaudits and hearts in France, Orville went
to Fort Myer just outside Washington, D.C., to conduct trials for the Signal Corps. His first flight was on September 3, 1908, and onlookers were
just as astounded as they had been in France. Orville went on to break several flight records for duration, height, and distance, some of which had just
been set by Wilbur in France. Then disaster struck. On September 17, while
carrying a passenger as required by the Signal Corps contract, a propeller on
Orville's Flyer split. The imbalance caused severe vibrations that loosened
the propeller bearings, and the wavering propeller cut one of the wires brac-
ing the rudder. The Flyer crashed from an altitude of about 50 feet. The
passenger, Lieutenant T.E. Selfridge, himself an amateur airplane builder,
was killed instantly. He was the first person killed in the history of powered
flight. Orville suffered a broken leg and hip injuries that caused him pain
until the end of his life.

Nonetheless, the Signal Corps was greatly impressed by what they had
seen before the crash. They drew up specifications for an aircraft to be sold
to the government after further trials in 1909. Orville went to France to be
with Wilbur, and at the end of 1908 Wilbur flew a Flyer seventy-seven miles
in just over two hours, breaking every flight record in the book, including
those they had set earlier in 1908. In many ways it was the high point in the
Wright brothers' aviation career.

On July 30, 1909, the government's required speed test was completed
and the United States calculated a payment for a Wright aircraft called
Columbia at $25,000 plus a $5,000 bonus for exceeding the minimum speed
requirement of 40 miles per hour. The actual speed was just over 42 miles
per hour. The brothers also collected fees well in excess of $40,000 in 1909
for other demonstration flights, and on November 22, 1909, the Wright Aircraft Company was formed by a group of investors. The brothers got $100,000

in cash, one-third of the stock, and a 10 percent royalty on each plane sold. The brothers had indeed cashed in on their invention. Further, the company was to bear the costs of pursuing suits for infringement of the patent held by the Wrights. Such suits also began in 1909.

In terms of profiting from their invention, 1909 represented the apex of the Wright brothers' career, just as their 1908 flights represented the high point in their flying exploits. Everything went downhill from there. Even though the brothers were victorious in courts of law, they were big losers in the court of public opinion. All the good will they had gained from their flying exploits drained away as they began to be perceived as money-grubbers who were trying to hold back progress. The patent fights were especially bitter with Glenn Curtiss, who in 1911 invented a seaplane that could operate on water as well as land, and who sold the first plane to the U.S. Navy. The court battles dragged on for seven long years until the U.S. Government, upon its entry into World War I in 1917, made all of the airplane manufacturers enter into cross-licensing agreements, and paid the Wright and Curtiss companies $2 million each for their trouble.

The Wright brothers' personal involvement also disappeared comparatively quickly. Wilbur died of typhoid fever in 1912, and Orville, who hated operating as a businessman rather than an inventor, sold out his interest in the company in 1915. At the end of the 1920s the companies merged into the Curtiss-Wright Corporation, but the bigger partner by far at that time was the Curtiss Company.

The hard fact was that the famous Flyer was nearly obsolete at the time of its great success in 1908 and 1909. The Wright brothers had erred in assuming they were much too far ahead of everyone to be caught, and the period that they spent selling instead of flying permitted many inventors to catch up. Certainly they and their Flyer flew much more adroitly than anyone else, but by the end of 1909, many pilots were doing just as well in a series of monoplanes (single wing aircraft) that had the added benefit of landing wheels. The famous Wright Flyer was no longer the best airplane in the air, and the death of Wilbur and virtual retirement of Orville removed the Wright brothers from the aeronautical scene in any significant way after 1915.

The arrival of the Douglas DC-3 in the 1930s marked the beginning of regular passenger travel in the airline industry (by 1939, the DC-3 was flying 90 percent of the world's airline passengers). In the decade following World War II, after the government had developed military jets, the advent of the Boeing 707 in 1954 marked the beginning of jet aircraft travel. The aircraft was originally called the "Dash-80" by employees of the company because Boeing had risked its own money to build the prototype, which they called the "367-80." At first, no one seemed to want the plane, but the military finally bought 29 freighters and Boeing went on to sell more than 800 planes, ultimately called the 707 series.

Boeing developed the 747 in 1970, and continued to be the most successful seller of jet airplanes through the 20th century. The jet made the airplane competitive in practically all markets, and the most popular transportation modes of the country became aircraft and automobiles. The automobile eliminated nearly all travel by rail in the 20th century, and the airplane was the only competing mode to really survive the automobile.

The Otto Internal Combustion Engine

The Wright brothers took the approach that as soon as they learned to control an aircraft, they would have no trouble developing a powered aircraft, because they planned to use the gasoline internal combustion engine. Several versions of the internal combustion engine had been developed in the 1800s, but it wasn't until Nikolaus August Otto of Germany developed a so-called air-breathing four-stroke version in 1876 that the internal combustion engine became a practical reality.

This engine produced a useful output of over 100 horsepower, even though it was reasonably light. Further development of the internal combustion engine gave the Wright brothers a leg up in their pursuit of manned flight, and also was the key to building the cheap, efficient cars of Henry Ford. In a real sense, the development of the internal combustion engine was as important to the transportation modes of the 20th century as the development of the steam engine had been to the transportation modes of the 19th century. The steam engine is still remembered today as the beginning of the Industrial Revolution, which it certainly was, but the development of the internal combustion engine was the basis for both the aircraft and automotive industries in the beginning of the 20th century, and should have received as much attention as the steam engine did in its day. The internal combustion engine, now looked upon with horror by most environmentalists, was probably the most important development of the 19th century in terms of changing the transportation modes of the United States from railroads to airplanes and automobiles.

Henry Ford and His Model T

The beginning of the automotive revolution dates back to the 1700s. A number of inventors tried to make versions of "horseless carriages," using steam engines modified for the purpose. In the 1880s electric car prototypes were made when electricity became widely used to run urban streetcars (trolley cars and the like). But it wasn't until the 1890s that cars based on the Otto

Internal Combustion Engine became quite successful, and so began America's love affair with the automobile.

The Dureya brothers of Massachusetts (once again, at first involved in the bicycle business) were nominally the first American inventors to sell a reasonable number of cars using the internal combustion engine. They first started producing them in quantity in 1896. Ransom Olds and his Oldsmobile company produced cars in good quantities near the turn of the century. Both were soon overtaken by the legendary car maker Henry Ford, who would go on to produce nearly half of the cars sold in the United States (and the world) for two decades beginning in 1908, in the process building over 15 million Model T cars between 1908 and 1927.

Ford was originally a farm boy, born in 1863, who delighted in things mechanical. After stints in Detroit as a teenage machinist and watch repairer, he went back to the farm at 19, and became a representative and repairman for farm machine companies. He returned to the city in 1891, now nearly 30 years old and a married man, to take a job with the Edison Illuminating Company, which provided the relatively new invention of electricity to Detroiters. Henry Ford became a superintendent there, with quite a bit of free time on his hands because he was very good at his job and his superiors tended to leave him alone.

In 1896, intrigued by the exploits of the Duryea brothers, Henry Ford started to build a gasoline-powered car of his own. In six months he had built what he called a Quadricycle, and was driving it around the streets of Detroit. By 1903 the Ford Motor Company was formed. It was actually the fourth business venture built around a Ford car. They had some successes in local races, including Barney Oldfield's famous "a mile a minute" run in 1902 (actually one minute and 1.2 seconds, still a new record), which was performed in a Ford car. However, the previous three ventures involving Ford had not been successful while he was still involved, largely because Ford couldn't stand being told what to do. But the Ford Motor Company succeeded beyond any of its founders' wildest dreams.

The company sold its first car, then dubbed the Model A, on July 15, 1903. The sale solved a very difficult cash flow problem for the company, and a deluge of orders followed. The company investors were very well pleased, because they essentially recouped their original investment within one year while maintaining ownership of a very promising company. But difficulties soon developed in deciding what part of the new automobile market to aim for: the high end, where profits per car were greater, or the lower end, where, hopefully, higher sales volume would more than make up for lower per-car profit. Car companies today face the same question.

This was one crucial difference between Henry Ford and the Wright brothers. Ford understood marketing as well as engineering, and he had a clear vision of how to address his market. He wanted to mass produce cars on one basic design for the mass market, driving down costs via economies of scale, which would permit him to constantly lower the price and increase his market share. By the end of 1905, Ford forced out the investors who disagreed with him by threatening to start another company. By the middle of 1906, he was the company's majority stock holder, and he was free to do as he pleased.

The secret of Henry Ford's subsequent overwhelming success was his single-minded pursuit of his vision. In 1907, he stated, "I will build a motor car for the great multitude. It will be large enough for the family, but small enough for the individual to run and care for. It will be constructed of the best materials, by the best men to be hired, after the simplest designs that modern engineering can devise. But it will be so low in price that no man making a good salary will be unable to own one — and enjoy with his family the blessing of hours of pleasure in God's great open spaces." Ford went on to do exactly that.

In the meantime the company was being supported by sales of new Ford cars, running through the alphabet to the Model N in 1906. By the end of the model year in September 1907 the Ford Motor Company had sold over eight thousand cars, almost five times their previous peak. The company also earned more than one million dollars in profit for the first time. The Model N was a smaller car, of the kind envisioned by Ford. The Models R and S were the result of some small changes, and helped the Model N support the company while Henry Ford and some key engineers went off to a small locked room in the factory in the winter of 1906-07 to invent the Model T.

It took them until the end of 1907, but in the spring of 1908 advance notice advertisements were sent to dealers. The Model T went on sale in October of 1908; at almost the same time Wilbur Wright became the toast of France for his flying exploits. The Model T was similarly a smashing success. Orders flooded in, until by the end of winter Ford had to announce they could not accept any more orders. They had enough to absorb the total output of the factory until August of 1909. By the end of the sales season in September 1909, Ford had sold more than 10,000 cars, a 60 percent increase over the prior year. Sales increased to over 700,000 by the 1916-17 sales year, then paused as the United States entered World War I. The 1920s started with over 900,000 sales, and the sales routinely began crossing the one million mark. In 1923, over two million units were sold, accounting for 57 percent of the cars produced in the United States, and just about half of the cars produced in the world. That was the peak production year, but what a peak. In terms of market penetration, the Model T has never been surpassed. In essence, it was the market.

The Model T's incredible market penetration explains the car's grip on the public. Everyone remembers his or her first car. In the case of nearly half the people in the United States, that first car was a Model T. For the 18 full calendar years from 1909 through 1926, the Model T averaged 42.9 percent of the market. It went over 50 percent six times, and in it captured 61.6 percent in 1921. In all, about 15.5 million Model T's were built, and it was estimated that almost 75 percent of those cars were still on the road when the Model T assembly line was shut down in 1927 to start work on a new model. The Model T led the nation (and usually the world) in sales 18 straight years, from 1909 through 1926.

The Model T was an instant success because of its great combination of advanced engineering features at a low price. The 1908 car was $825, not the cheapest on the market, but the cheapest that included so many desirable features. The car would sell for $440 in 1914 and $345 in 1916, and reach an all-time low of $290 in 1925, as Ford perfected the moving assembly line and car sales boomed. This was a price level that no one could match, and Henry Ford came close capturing 100 percent of the "low cost" market before the Model T became obsolete in the late 1920s. Ford operated by a simple concept, but one hard to accomplish, stating: "Every time you reduce the price of the car without reducing the quality, you increase the possible number of purchasers. There are many men who will pay $360 for a car who would not pay $440. We had in round numbers 500,000 buyers of cars on the $440 basis, and I figure that on the $360 basis we can increase the sales to possibly 800,000 cars for the year—less profit on each car, but more cars, more employment of labor, and in the end we get all the profit we ought to make."

Henry Ford did not take patents on either his cars or the moving assembly line process he created to build them in such high quantities—first in Highland Park and later in the factory he built on the River Rouge. Everybody was free to attempt to compete with him, using his ideas. This was opposite of the approach taken by the Wright brothers. A patent lawyer named George Selden, who never built an operable car nor intended to, managed to get a patent issued in 1895 on what he guessed a successful car would involve. He later sold his patent to a company hoping to make money from pressing claims, from which Selden would get a royalty. Early car manufacturers fell in line rather than pay to defend the suits, but when Henry Ford was sued in 1903 he told Selden what he could do with his patent. The suit dragged on until 1909, when Selden won an initial decision, but Ford appealed and won an overwhelming victory in 1911.

Ford became a folk hero with his victory, and as he was pressing on to make a car available to everyone, not just the rich, he would largely be forgiven for the many mistakes he would make later when he turned his attention away from cars and towards politics, among other things. Ford forced out his remaining shareholders by again threatening to build a competing company, and they sold out to him by the middle of 1919. Now Henry Ford and his family owned the Ford Motor Company lock, stock, and barrel. But with no one to tell him when he was wrong, Henry Ford began to act irrationally in many ways. He refused to accept criticism, and adamantly refused to change the Model T, even though the Chevrolet division of General Motors began to nip at his heels.

In 1926, Ford's market share was only 34 percent and falling (a low value only in comparison to Ford's glory years). The Chevrolet division of a reorganized General Motors company had been second to Ford in the five years from 1922 through 1926, as Chevrolet sales increased from 200,000 to 590,000. The Model T was almost 20 years old, and the car-buying public was now interested in the yearly changes they got in engineering and styling from Chevrolet (and most other cars by then). Faced with the new challenge from Chevrolet, Henry Ford finally decided to build a new model. On May 26, 1927, it was announced that the assembly line would soon shut down to retool for a new model. This was just after Henry Ford and his son Edsel drove the fifteen millionth Model T off the assembly line. The Model T, which truly launched the automobile business in the United States, was about to cease production. A car with its impact upon the business and its market would never be seen again.

Chevrolet finally overtook Ford in sales in 1927 with the Ford assembly line shut down, and overall sales in 1927 fell by about one million units as buyers waited to see what Ford would come up with. They were not disappointed. On December 2, 1927, Ford officially unveiled its new Model A. People crowded showrooms to see the new car, and it was estimated that 25 million people — about 20 percent of the nation's population — came out to see the car in its first week on display. And they did not just come to look. About half a million firm orders were taken by Christmas, and each one was accompanied by a full deposit. The price of the new Model A was $495, still a car for the masses, and actually a little cheaper pound-for-pound than the somewhat lighter Model T. The new Model A had all the improvements most in demand at the time, and with sales of 1.5 million cars in 1929, Ford regained the sales lead over Chevrolet, capturing a market share of 34 percent, compared to 20 percent for the Chevrolet.

But the Model A was a one-year wonder. Chevrolet came back with a redesigned model to retake the lead in 1930, and Ford's days as the industry leader were over. The Chevrolet was the product of a well-run corporation that would dominate the car market of the United States and the world for the rest of the century. Ford was a company in disarray, and almost went bankrupt under Henry Ford's autocratic rule, and the U.S. Government called grandson Henry Ford II home from the Navy to save the company — and its government contracts — in the 1940s. It has been said that out of Ford in the 1920s came a new car, with great travail. Out of General Motors in the 1920s came the model of a professional, modern corporation. Just as everyone copied Henry Ford's assembly line manufacturing techniques, everyone — but Ford — copied the management techniques that General Motors developed in the 1920s.

The world grew to prefer the automotive mode of transportation after 1908 (just as aircraft transportation grew dramatically following the deeds of the Wright brothers in 1908). It is notable that the two companies that really created the automotive industry — Ford and General Motors — are still the two biggest automobile companies in the world today. There were more than 500 companies created to pursue the automotive business between 1900 and 1908, but most disappeared along the way. William C. (Billy) Durant, probably the second most seminal figure in the business after Henry Ford, created General Motors in 1908, although he lost it in 1910, got it back in 1916 after acquiring Chevrolet, and then lost it for good in 1920 when the Du Ponts and Albert Sloan arrived on the scene to lead General Motors into its bright future. Also, a young engineer named Charles Kettering, an employee of National Cash Register, started experimenting on improved automobile ignition systems in a barn in 1908. The barn became Delco Corporation, where Kettering later invented the electrical starting system. Delco was eventually bought by General Motors, and Kettering went on to invent many other items. Without a doubt, 1908 was the year two key new modes of transportation, the airplane and the automobile, began their roles as the preferred methods of transportation in the United States. By the same token, 1908 effectively marked the beginning of the end for the railroads, and all other forms of mass transportation via rails. Not only had railroads seemed invincible as the 1900s dawned, but city transportation systems using rails and railway cars such as the trolley car, the interurban lines, elevated systems, and subways seemed to be the wave of the future. All were severely affected by the preference for private and public forms of automotive travel. Only air travel was destined to grow, together with the automotive business, in the 1900s.

The Slow Death of Travel by Rail

A basic reason for the triumph of automotive transportation over all forms of rail transportation after 1900 was the fact that the federal and local governments invested a great deal of capital in building roads. Cars and trucks were favored as a highly popular way to stop the monopolistic practices of the railroads. In the meantime, local railed transportation systems essentially strangled themselves by signing franchise agreements that required them to keep fares constant, though overhead rose due to inflation and higher labor costs as unions gained power in the 1930s. The railroads were reaping the rewards of public displeasure, left over from the days when they raised costs unmercifully because they were the only game in town.

As noted earlier, the Grange movement of the 1870s and the anti-trust efforts in Washington led to the formation of the Interstate Commerce Commission in 1887 in an attempt to control the railroads. Unfavorable Supreme Court decisions made the Interstate Commerce Commission largely ineffective until 1907, when a favorable Supreme Court ruling permitted the commission to set maximum rates. This was the beginning of an adverse regulation atmosphere for the railroads that would eventually lead to their essential demise.

In 1916, railroads were still carrying 98 percent of all passenger traffic, but several were in trouble, although they acted as arrogantly as ever. In January of 1917, President Wilson signed the Adamson Act, which imposed the 8-hour day on the railroads. On Wilson's Inauguration Day on March 5, 1917 (the last time a President used a horse and carriage to lead the Inauguration Procession — it was automobiles after that), Wilson all but declared the nation's entry into World War I, a declaration he made official within a month, and the issue of mobilizing troops and getting them to East Coast embarkation points arose. Railroads were still acting as if cooperating with the government was beneath them, even though they were in some disarray due to the increased taxes and regulations that had been imposed on them in the last 15 years. A furious Wilson seized control of the railroads by the end of 1917.

In contrast, the automotive industry was anxious to help. To help relieve the railroads, they drove thirty thousand trucks bound for the European front from their Midwestern plants eastward in the midst of an unusually severe winter, over clearly inadequate roads. From 1917 onward billions were poured into better roads, culminating in the Interstate Highway Act signed by President Eisenhower in 1956. During the same time, railroads would be saddled with ever more regulations, so that, except for a resurgence during World War II due to limitations on automobile use, their markets were overtaken by cars, trucks, and even airplanes. The railroads would become largely obsolete. In a debate in the Senate around 1930, it was said that the railroads have had their day, but if they did not exist no one would see a reason now for inventing them.

The same was true for mass transit systems using rail, but the detailed reasons were somewhat different, even though the basic reason was the same in both cases — the growing popularity of the private automobile, and the growing number of miles of good roads to drive them on. Streetcars, essentially copied from the railroads, became popular in the late 1800s. They were originally pulled by horses, which added a great deal of manure to the crowded cities. But in the 1880s, Frank Sprague developed a system in Richmond, Virginia, that would operate on electricity. Sprague had spent some time working with Thomas Edison in his laboratories in Menlo Park, and he was determined to electrify streetcars and eliminate horses and the mess they created from the traffic in cities. Sprague demonstrated his system to leading officials from Boston in 1888, and the officials decided that Boston would use Sprague's electrical system. That began the electrification of streetcar systems across the country.

These streetcar systems were known as mass transit, but they were not considered rapid transit, which was a system with its own right-of-way and no involvement with the traffic in the streets. Rapid transit systems were limited to either those that were elevated above the street, or to subways that ran beneath the street. Boston and New York were the first two big cities to build subways, at the turn of the century, and several cities built elevated systems, known as "the El" on the East Coast or the "L" in Chicago. By using electrification, these systems avoided the need for a steam engine, with its associated smoke.

But all of these systems would eventually fail, because, as in the past, in order to gain a franchise in a given city the builder would have to essentially agree never to increase the fare. People still had bad memories of the railroads and their abuses during the days of their monopoly. All of the railed systems built late in the 1800s and early in the 1900s peaked around World War I, and then began to experience problems with increasing costs. It soon became clear that the only way the systems could remain in operation would be if the various cities, or municipalities, took over their operation. That way, the capital costs of the system could be paid for by bonds or other such municipal funding, and the fare hopefully would be enough to pay the operating costs. However, the fare never was enough, and the municipalities had to choose between operating the systems at a loss, or, the politically unpopular option of raising the fare. The New York subway system, for example, kept its nickel fare into the 1950s, before they decided to increase the fare to cover the increased operating costs. That fare today is $2.00, quite an increase from the nickel fare that existed for many decades.

As travel by automobile became more popular, fewer and fewer people used the streetcar and the subway systems. The problem became even worse when companies began to locate in the suburbs, where many people had moved. This meant that many workers never needed to go into the city at all for any purpose, except perhaps for "nights out on the town" when they tended to prefer to drive anyhow. In World War II, when driving was limited, railed transportation systems, including the railroad, had great peaks in demand, but it was really their final hurrah. As soon as World War II was over, people continued a mass exodus from the cities to the suburbs. Roads were built to accommodate the shift and by the end of the 1950s, the preferred transportation mode across the nation was the car, or perhaps airplanes for longer trips.

So in essence, 1908 marked the beginning of the end of large-scale transportation via any type of vehicle that operated on rails. By the end of the 1900s, railroads were obsolete and the only railway travel into big cities was via systems that were subsidized by the cities. There have been some attempts to build new subways in large, metropolitan areas in order to improve driving conditions, but all of these subways operate with support from the local government. Automobile travel has, in a sense, become untenable in large, metropolitan areas because there are simply too many cars trying to use limited roadways. The preferred method of transportation everywhere is via car. For example, attempts to get people to carpool in the Los Angeles area by creating extra lanes on the freeway for vehicles with two or more occupants have been a complete failure. People generally insist on driving their own cars, by themselves, and they will have nothing to do with carpooling systems. Attempts by cities to ignore this fact, and to make drivers behave differently, have constantly failed. Future plans for improved transportation in and around cities need to accept the fact that people will drive into the cities by themselves, rather than taking part in any kind of carpooling. Rail systems, no matter how new or modern, can only go where the rails go. Busses still must use regular streets. The result is ongoing traffic jams that have become a way of life, and that will probably be a permanent feature of metropolitan driving. There is no doubt as to what mode of transportation is now a permanent fixture of American life. Americans prefer to drive.

A Brief History of Mail Transportation

It is instructive to look at the history of mail delivery by the nation's Postal Service to demonstrate the use of different modes of transportation throughout the nation's history. Every available mode has been used at different times, and it was the Post Office Department that gave life to most airlines early in their careers by giving them contracts to carry the mail. Further, it was the Post Office's decision to begin Rural Free Delivery (RFD) that gave a great boost to the creation of roads in the nation.

Between the Revolution in 1776 and the First World War the United States Post Office tried a number of different kinds of transportation to deliver the mail. The Post Office was always one of the first official organizations to try new modes of transportation. It was beneficial both for the Post Office, in terms of getting more rapid delivery of the mail, and it was beneficial to the new mode of transportation, in terms of being able to get some revenue to get the new mode up and running. So the mail delivery evolved in lock-step with the modes of transportation from foot, to horseback, stagecoach, steamboat, railroad, automobile and airplane. The Post Office even experimented with the use of balloons, helicopters, and pneumatic tubes. They were not always successful with a new mode of transportation, but they certainly gave support to it, and help draw public attention to it.

Early in the 1800s, the Post Office had purchased a number of stage-coaches for operation on the nation's better post roads (a post road was any road on which the mail traveled; usually, but not necessarily, one of the best roads in the region). Thus the old Boston Post Road is known to many people in New England, without conscious thought being given to the fact that the road was so designated because it carried mail. In 1823, the Post Office declared many waterways as post roads, even though it had already been using steamboats to carry mail between towns where no roads existed for a good ten years.

In 1831, steam-driven engines had been described by some people as "traveling at the unconscionable speed of 15 miles per hour" and many people said they were "a device of Satan to lead immortal souls to hell." The Post Office braved public disfavor by beginning to carry mail on railroads for short distances. By 1836, the Postal Service had awarded its first mail contracts to the railroads, and two years later railroads were designated post roads. As early as 1896 — the beginning of serious automotive experimental activity — the Post Office was experimenting with what they called the "horse-less wagon" to carry the mail, both more quickly and cheaply. In 1899, the Post Office was experimenting with a system for delivering the mail by automobile out of Buffalo, New York and in 1901, it signed its first contract to carry the mail between Buffalo and a postal station in the Pan-American Exposition grounds, about four and half miles away, by automobile. On January 1, 1902, they started mail delivery via automotive services in Minneapolis.

The Post Office continued to write contracts for delivery by automobile between 1901 and 1914, but they felt they were being charged exorbitant rates, and some of the contracts involved fraud. As a result, the department asked for and received approval from Congress to establish the first government-owned vehicle service, at Washington, D.C., starting on October 19, 1914.

One of the most romanticized episodes in Post Office history was the development of mail delivery via Pony Express. The population of the western part of the United States began to grow rapidly after gold was discovered in California in 1848, and the only way to get mail to the Pacific Coast was via ship to Panama, across Panama by rail, and then on to San Francisco via another ship. It was supposed to take three to four weeks to receive a letter from the East, but they rarely managed to deliver mail that rapidly.

Californians felt especially isolated, as it took more than six weeks for the people in Los Angeles to learn that California had been admitted to the Union. In 1853, Los Angeles newspapers were complaining that four weeks had gone by since they had had a delivery of mail. They said that the mail rider comes and goes regularly, but not the mailbags. Sometimes the mail didn't arrive in San Diego, where it was taken by donkey up to Los Angeles, and sometimes there was so much mail that it was sent to San Pedro by steamer, then shipped it up to San Francisco, and finally, much later, to Los Angeles. By 1860, there was immense pressure to find a more rapid method of mail delivery.

In March of 1860, a businessman named William H. Russell placed the following advertisement, a classic piece of history, in selected newspapers: "Wanted: Young, skinny, wiry fellows, not over 18. Must be expert riders willing to risk death daily. Orphans preferred." Russell was planning to develop a mail service for an express route to carry mail between St. Josephs, Missouri — then the westernmost point reached by the railroad and telegraph — and California. There was practically nothing between St. Josephs and the West, except for a few forts and settlements, on the 2,000-mile route. There were a great deal of Indians in the area at that time, many of whom were hostile to white men. Russell had tried, without success, to get a contract for his service from the Senate Post Office in Washington, D.C. He was unsuccessful, because most people thought Russell's idea was, to put the best face on it, simply impossible.

Russell and two partners formed the Central Overland California and Pike's Peak Express Company. They built a number of relay stations and improved existing ones for use in the delivery service. The country was combed for good horses to carry the riders being recruited via the newspaper ads. The riders, in spite of the dangers of the job for which they were being recruited, had to swear on the Bible not to cuss, fight, or abuse their animals, and to conduct themselves honestly.

Starting on April 13, 1860, the Pony Express ran through parts of Missouri, Kansas, Nebraska, Colorado, Wyoming, Utah, Nevada, and California. On an average day a rider traveled 75 to 100 miles. He changed horses at relay stations set about ten miles apart, transferring himself and his *mochilla* (a saddle cover with four pockets, or *cantinas,* for mail) to the new mount, all in one quick leap.

The first mail by Pony Express via the central route from St. Joseph to Sacramento took ten and half days, cutting the Overland Stage time via the southern route by more than half. The fastest delivery was in March 1861, when President Lincoln's Inaugural Address was carried in seven days and seventeen hours, which is ironic when one considers that Lincoln was a major force in initiating the building of the transcontinental railroad just a year later.

The Pony Express only operated from April of 1860, to October 24, 1861. For the last four months of its operation, it was officially under contract to the Post Office, rather than a private enterprise. When the transcontinental telegraph line was completed in 1861, the Pony Express went out of business. It only existed for about 18 months, but tales have been told about the Pony Express ever since.

The Post Office began carrying mail via railroad as soon as railroads became widespread in the 1830s. On July 7, 1838, Congress passed an act designating all railroads in the United States as post routes. As a result mail service by railroad increased rapidly for the rest of the century. In June of 1840, two mail agents were appointed to accompany the mail from Boston to Springfield "to make exchanges of mail, attend to delivery, and receive and forward all unpaid way letters and packages received." This was the start of sorting mail on the railroad lines instead of only in post offices. Gradually, the clerks began to make up mail for connecting lines, as well as local offices, as the idea of distributing all transit mail on the cars slowly evolved.

The first experiment in delivering U.S. mail in "post offices on wheels" was made in 1862, between Hannibal and St. Joseph, Missouri. On August 28, 1864, the first U.S. Railroad Post Office Route was officially established, when a postal car equipped for general distribution was placed in service between Chicago and Clinton, Iowa. Similar routes were established on other lines. By 1930, more than 10,000 trains were used to move the mail into every city, town, and village in the United States. However, following passage of the Transportation Act of 1958, mail transport via passenger trains declined rapidly. By 1965, only 190 trains carried mail, and by 1970, the railroad carried virtually no first-class mail. This demonstrates the rapidity with which the railroads lost business to the new modes of automobile and airplane transportation.

In the early part of the 19th century, envelopes were not used for delivering mail. Instead, a letter was folded and the address placed on the outside of the sheet. The customer had to take a letter to the post office to mail it, and the addressee had to pick up the letter at the post office, unless he or she lived in one of about forty big cities where a carrier would deliver it to the home address for an extra penny or two. Postage stamps became available in 1847, and at that time, mailers had the option of sending their letters and having the recipients pay the postage. But by 1855, prepayment became compulsory. In 1858, street boxes for mail collection began to appear, and in 1863, free city delivery was instituted in 49 of the country's largest cities. By

1890, 454 post offices were delivering mail to residents of the United States' cities. It was not until the turn of the century, however, that free delivery came to farmers and other rural residents. The initiation of rural free delivery (RFD) was crucial to the development of roads in the United States.

It is difficult today to envision the isolation in which most farm families lived in early America. The farmers' main link to the outside world, before telephones, radios, and television were common, was the mail and the newspapers that came by mail to the nearest post office. Since the mail had to be picked up, this meant a trip to the post office, often involving a day's travel round-trip; a farmer might delay picking up the mail for days, weeks, or even months until the trip could be coupled with picking up food, supplies, or equipment.

A member of a famous retail family, John Wanamaker of Pennsylvania, was the first postmaster general to advocate RFD. Although funds were appropriated a month before he left office in 1893, subsequent postmasters general dragged their feet on inaugurating the new service, so that it was 1896 before the first experimental rural delivery routes began in West Virginia, with carriers working out of post offices in Charleston, Halltown, and Uvila.

In the history of the Post Office, many transportation innovations were marked by great demonstrations, including the beginning of the Pony Express and scheduled airmail service in 1918. However, the West Virginia experiment with RFD was launched in relative obscurity, and in an atmosphere of hostility. Many critics claimed that RFD was impractical and too expensive. A post carrier trudging over rutted roads and through forests, trying to deliver mail in all kinds of weather, seemed silly to the critics.

But the farmers, without exception, were delighted with the new service. After receiving free delivery for a few months, one observed it would take away part of his life to give it up. A Missouri farmer looked back and calculated that in 15 years, he had traveled 12,000 miles going to and from his Post Office to get the mail. Politicians normally listen to such positive feedback on subjects upon which they might be called to vote, and the critics were pushed aside. No politician was going to create enemies of farmers, who at the time made up the largest single block of the population. Even the powerful railroads did not have as many employees as the number of people engaged in agricultural work.

So RFD continued and was expanded. It was a powerful stimulant to the development of better roads and highways. In this sense, critics were correct, but no one was willing to stand up and say they were opposed to better roads in general, and RFD for farmers specifically. After hundreds of petitions for rural delivery were turned down by the Post Office because of unserviceable and inaccessible roads, local governments began to extend and improve existing highways. Between 1897 and 1908, these local governments spent an estimated $72 million on bridges, culverts, and other improvements. In one county in Indiana, farmers themselves paid over $2,600 to grade and gravel a road in order to qualify for RFD. Looking back now, the impact of RFD as a cultural and social agent of change for millions of Americans cannot be overestimated. It is difficult for us to see today what the fuss was all about. RFD is such an established service linking industrial and rural America that it is hard to imagine the lack of such a service. Many companies went into the catalog business simply because the large number of farmers in the country were now accessible at low cost. The rapid growth of roads in the first few decades of the century was an important reason why Henry Ford was able, almost single-handedly, to create the automobile industry with the Model T. There have been many critics, who were friendly to the idea of rail travel, who claimed that there was a "conspiracy" between the government and the automobile business to create new roads. But there is no doubt that the economic growth of the United States in the 20th century was very much due to the creation of a national network of good roads. People can bemoan the loss of a simpler, less complicated time when there were far fewer automobiles in the world, but constantly yearning for the past is not the way to make a positive contribution to a brighter future.

For 1,800 years, between the height of the Roman Empire and the world of 1800, there was very little change in modes of transportation. In the 19th century, there was *one* major change in transportation modes, and that of course was the railroad. In the 20th century, there were *two* major changes, the automobile and the airplane, and all of the infrastructure changes that came with them in terms of highways and airports. We are still living in that time of great change in the modes of transportation, but in the United States and the world. There is no doubt that the great economic growth of the United States in the 20th century has been supported by the birth of the automotive and airline industries. Certainly there were greater changes in the ways in which people traveled in the 1900s than in the 1,900 years that went before. There may be equally great changes in the 21st century, but they are not yet on the horizon. Probably the year 1908 will never be repeated in terms of the development of transportation that took place in that single year. But, as always, it is hard to see how the future will develop. It is always necessary to realize that if great technological changes have just recently taken place, then it is probable that further great technological changes will continue to occur. There is no way to say what shape those changes will take, but you can be sure they will occur. In our age, the only constant is change.

CHRONOLOGY OF TRANSPORTATION

The major events in the chronology of transportation in the United States (and the world) were the development of the steam engine in 1769 (which led to the development of the steam locomotive and the railroads by 1830) and the events of the year of 1908, when Henry Ford sold his first Model T and the Wright Brothers demonstrated their ability to fly, astounding large crowds in France and the United States.

Very little happened to change modes of transportation in a substantial way in the first 1800 years of the millennium, until the railroads changed everything in the early 1800s. The year 1908 marked the real beginning of transportation via automobile and airplane, and the subsequent changes in transportation that took place in the 20th century were greater than those that had occurred in the previous 1900 years.

This chronology begins with the establishment of a postal service in the colonies, an event in any country that helps in the development of roads and communication. Other events related to primitive transportation which should not be ignored were taking place in the colonies while James Watt was inventing the steam engine, which would lead to the first great changes in transportation since the time of the Roman Empire. In this way, one can best appreciate how great were the changes created by the coming of the railroad, and subsequently the coming of the automobile and the airplane.

December 10, 1672— New York and Massachusetts agreed to start a monthly postal service between New York City and Boston. An announcement was made on this date by Governor Francis Lovelace of New York that the service would be inaugurated on January 1 of 1673, but the first trip was not made until January 22, 1673. In this way, postal service in the colonies was started twenty years before the official creation of a Post Office system by the English Parliament.

April 4, 1692— The British Postmaster General confirmed Andrew Hamilton as postmaster general of the American colonies. A royal patent had been granted over one year earlier, on February 17, 1691, to create such a post office, but it was not until April of 1692 that a postmaster general for the colonies was named. By then, the colonies had already established some postal routes of their own.

November 9, 1756— The first regularly scheduled inter-city stagecoach service was started between New York City and Philadelphia. This was a significant route because Philadelphia was the largest and most important city of colonial times, and New York was a rapidly growing number two. As early as the 1730s "stage wagons" had been running across New Jersey, and in 1785 they would begin running between New York and Albany. Perhaps most notable of all would be the "flying machine" that would begin running between New York and Philadelphia in 1771.

The "flying machine" offered public transportation between the two cities in only a day and a half (in good weather) with overnight lodging provided as required. It offered high speed and the state of the art in terms of equipment and comfort. Stagecoaches were typically drawn by four or six horses, which were changed en route, and on reasonable roads they averaged 3–5 miles per hour. The building of stagecoaches and wagons and carriages of all kinds became an important industry in the United States, and developed a trained cadre of artisans who would play an important role in the evolution of transportation. The famous Conestoga wagons, originating in the Conestoga River Valley in Pennsylvania, began to appear around 1725 and were being built by the thousands by the time the Revolutionary War started.

September, 1769— James Watt, a Scottish inventor, completed his repair of a steam engine, which was later patented. Watt was working as an instrument maker at the University of Glasgow when he was asked to repair a model of a steam engine that had been developed by James Newcombe (which in turn was a modification of prior designs). Watt made so many improvements that the result of his efforts has been generally considered the first practicable steam engine. The basic unit of power, the watt, is named after James Watt.

Versions of steam engines, as noted above, had been designed prior to the one completed by Watt, but his was the first that could run by itself and run other machines as well. It was the cornerstone of the Industrial Revolution, and even if we limit its applications to the field of transportation, it was the basis for the steam locomotive that led to the railroad; it was the basis for steamships; and it was also the basis of early automobiles, which were powered by the steam engine. The steam engine today exists primarily in the form of steam turbines, which produce most of the electricity in the world. It seems ironic that electricity, which replaced the steam engine in so many applications, is itself produced mainly by the steam turbine.

January 24, 1776— John Adams and two friends began a trip from Boston to Philadelphia, with a stop in Cambridge to talk with General Washington. Adams planned to once more join the Continental Congress in Philadelphia, and to bring news of the status of the conflict between General Washington and the British, then embroiled in battle as the British continued their occupation of Boston and their blockade of Boston Harbor. The Continental Congress of 1776, with Adams continuing to press for independence as a delegate from his home state of Massachusetts, would later issue the Declaration of Independence. The trip Adams and his friends began in January of that year illustrates the realities of transportation in colonial days. The trip required a total of 15 days, and the travelers did not arrive in Philadelphia until February 8, 1776, averaging just over 25 miles per day on their journey.

They traveled via the post road west across Massachusetts (as noted before, the designation "post road" meant simply that the road was used to deliver mail — it was no indication of the quality of the road, although post roads were usually among the best) from the Boston area to Springfield, then crossed the Connecticut River by ferry, and followed the river bank south into Connecticut. At Wethersfield (south of Hartford) they left the riverbank to join the New Haven Road, and upon reaching the New Haven area they proceeded along the Connecticut shore through Fairfield, Norwalk, Stamford, and Greenwich, after which they picked up the New York Post Road. Once they reached the northern suburbs of the City of New York, they were ferried across the Hudson River to New Jersey, where Adams, who had once been surveyor of roads in his hometown of Braintree, felt the roads were unusually good. There were three more ferry crossings, at Hackensack, Newark, and New Brunswick, before they got nearly on a straight line to Philadelphia. They went through the small college town of Princeton, and on into Trenton where the mighty Delaware River loomed. Another ferry ride took them into Pennsylvania, only twenty miles north of Philadelphia.

They went through more than 50 towns en route, a necessary itinerary because they had to stop several times a day to eat, sleep, and tend the horses. They were lucky that ice, which could clog the rivers, did not interfere with their many ferry crossings. This was a typical trip in the colonies at that time.

No one could imagine that in less than 75 years the railroad would make such a trip a pleasant journey, while reducing the travel time to the order of one day.

March 2, 1776— Another journey that demonstrated the realities of transportation around the time of the Revolution ended on this day. In 1775, a group of New Englanders under Ethan Allen had taken over Fort Ticonderoga, near what was then the western border of Massachusetts, in New York. Although it was considered impossible by most, they undertook to bring back the various cannons and pieces of artillery from Fort Ticonderoga and deliver them to Boston in the winter of 1776. The big problem was dragging all of this artillery over the Berkshire Mountains. It was an especially severe winter, but that actually helped the soldiers, because they could drag the guns over the snow on sleighs. Just before Adams began his trip to Philadelphia, the guns had arrived in Framingham, Massachusetts, a few miles west of Boston.

In one night's very quiet work the guns were moved onto the heights of Dorchester, which overlooked the Boston harbor. On this date, the British found out the guns were in Dorchester, and cannonballs began to rain down upon their positions in Boston over the next few days. Reportedly, the Boston commander, on seeing the guns up on the heights of Dorchester, remarked, "My god! These fellows have done more work in one night than I can make my army do in three months." Finally, on Sunday, March 17, St. Patrick's Day, the British began abandoning Boston and the entire fleet of ships sailed out into the open sea. A deal had been struck between the Americans and General William Howe of the British that if the British were allowed to depart in peace, they would not leave Boston in flames. Soon after, the Duke of Manchester arose in the House of Lords in London to complain "the army which was sent to reduce the province of Massachusetts Bay has been driven from the capital, and the standard of the provincial army now waved in triumph over the walls of Boston." As it turned out, the British fleet returned later in the year as part of a larger armada sailing from England, after the Declaration of Independence had been issued and the Revolutionary War had officially started, and the combined fleet attacked New York and inflicted painful initial losses on the colonies. But that was in the future, and in March of 1776 there was only joy in the colonies.

Most people assumed it was impossible to transport the guns from Fort Ticonderoga over the Berkshire Mountains to Boston. Although this chronology is about the major improvements that were made in transportation mostly in the 200 years following the Revolutionary War, it has to be remembered that it is not impossible for men of spirit to undertake great endeavors in transporting crucial materials over seemingly impassable roads. There is a Chinese saying to the effect that a journey of 10,000 miles begins with but a single step.

This lesson was forgotten by the French in Vietnam in 1954. They had established a fortified camp at a place called Dien Bien Phu. It was pointed out to the French commander that if guns were placed in the hills above the command, the French could be massacred. The commander responded that "those people" would never be able to drag guns and artillery through the jungle and up into the hills. Of course, "those people" did just that using their backs and where possible, animals. The French were driven out of Dien Bien Phu and Vietnam, just as the British were driven out of Boston in 1776.

Before the railroads' arrival in the early 1800s, America was settled by people who undertook "impossible" journeys in the primitive transportation conditions of the time. While railroads, automobiles, and airplanes permitted people to move around at will, without the spirit of adventure and the urge for mobility shown by most Americans, the country would not have been successfully settled in such a short time, regardless of the means of transportation available.

December 14, 1793— Kentucky was the first state to authorize commissioners to raise money for the purpose of building a road. This was an important step because state and local governments had been notoriously unwilling or unable to raise the money to improve the generally terrible roads in the new United States. In Kentucky and elsewhere, when the state or local government did not provide funds, entrepreneurs stepped in to fill the urgent need. In this situation, they proposed toll roads.

The first toll road in the United States had been attempted by Virginia in 1785, but the road was not surfaced and was completely worn out by 1795. The first toll road to be built and operated by a private company was the Philadelphia and Lancaster turnpike chartered by Pennsylvania in 1792. It was a complete success and was the start of a turnpike-building frenzy in the United States. It was 62 miles long, 37 feet wide, and was paved with stone and covered with gravel. It was at once crowded with traffic, and as the dividends rolled in, it was extended roughly 15 more miles to the Susquehanna River.

Other states quickly jumped on the bandwagon. The Catskill Turnpike was done before 1804, and the Mohawk and Hudson turnpike running west from Albany soon followed. By 1821 New York had 4,000 miles of turnpikes, and Pennsylvania and Massachusetts both had chartered nearly 150 turnpike companies. Baltimore had risen to be the third largest city in the States thanks in large part to its seven trunk-line turnpikes, and the famous Shenandoah Valley turnpike in Virginia, 92 miles long, carried heavy traffic. Around this period, the peak of turnpike building in the early United States, the so-called

National Road — intended to run 700 miles from Maryland into Illinois, then the far west — was born, and began carrying traffic on an August day in 1817. Ironically, this frenzy of road building would soon come to an end because of competition from canals and railroads. It would be another century before road building started in earnest once again.

August 17, 1807 — Robert Fulton, an American inventor and engineer who was born near Lancaster, Pennsylvania, teamed up with financier Robert R. Livingston to build the first practical steamship to operate in American waters, which he sailed on the Hudson River on this date. Livingston held a monopoly on steamboat navigation on the Hudson, and on this day Fulton's ship, later called the *Clermont* after Livingston's estate, was launched. The ship was equipped with a steam engine built by the Birmingham, England, company of Boulton and Watt. It was 133 feet long and driven by a pair of paddle wheels that were 15 feet in diameter. The *Clermont* made the voyage up the Hudson to Albany and back at an average speed of five knots. It took about 62 hours to make the 240-mile trip, one that average sailing ships would take as long as 96 hours to complete.

The *Clermont* began regular passenger service to Albany in September. Like Watt's steam engine, a number of men had built steamboats before Fulton (including John Fitch and William Symington), but Fulton built the first one to be commercially successful in American waters, and thus he is remembered as the inventor of the steamship. Fulton went on to design several other ships, including a steam warship. Fulton also established a steamship ferryboat service in New York City which replaced the sailboat ferries that dated back to Revolutionary times. Joined by others, the ferry service expanded to 70 steamboats by the end of the Civil War. Some still operate today.

By 1811, Nicholas Roosevelt was running a paddlewheel steamboat up and down the Mississippi, going from Pittsburgh to New Orleans in 14 days. Standard boats on the Mississippi at that time took about 40 days to cover the same distance, and operating such ships against the current on the return trip could take 75 to 90 days. Steamships soon were everywhere on the Mississippi.

October 26, 1825 — The Erie Canal officially opened on this date, and proved to be a great boon to the growth of New York City and upstate New York. The canal connected the Hudson River at Albany to Buffalo on Lake Erie, thus establishing a waterway between the port of New York City and the Midwest via the Great Lakes. Lake Erie was 550 feet above the level of tidewater on the Hudson, and the canal was 360 miles long. It was 40 feet wide at Buffalo and 28 feet wide at its end, with an average depth of only four feet. It took about nine million dollars and eight years to build it, but proved well worth the cost and trouble when it opened.

Often derided as De Witt Clinton's "Big Ditch" in semi-honor of the man who pushed the hardest to get the canal funded and started, the Erie Canal was so successful, as toll roads had been before it, that it started a spate of canal building in the United States. Much shorter canals had been built beginning in 1785, but nothing near the scale of the Erie Canal, which itself was extended into different areas of New York state after it was officially opened.

Ironically, the same year the Erie Canal was officially opened for business (short stretches were in use earlier), John Stevens of Hoboken, New Jersey, built and operated the first experimental steam locomotive in the United States. In 1830, the Baltimore & Ohio Railroad began carrying its first revenue-producing passengers. The Tom Thumb, the first fully operational steam locomotive produced in the United States, was built in 1829 for the Baltimore and Ohio. The railroad was funded in preference to a proposed canal from Baltimore westward meant to compete with the Erie Canal. The railroads were coming fast, and they would eventually put all of the canals out of business. For about 75 years the dominance of the railroads meant that the construction of better roads was largely unnecessary, but that would change as soon as the automobile made its appearance.

February 28, 1827 — The Baltimore & Ohio Railroad Company was incorporated, and the age of the railroad in the United States was underway. After going through the appropriate legal steps and state approvals, construction began with a huge celebration on July 4, 1828. Nearly every citizen of Baltimore owned at least one share of stock in the new company.

The railroad emerged as the preferred choice of investors also considering a canal from Baltimore to the Ohio River to compete with the Erie Canal. Baltimore had grown to a population of 60,000 in the 1820s, making it the third-largest city in the nation. A connection between Baltimore and the Ohio River was needed to offset the advantage that New York City had gained with the construction of the Erie Canal. A potential investor, Evan Thomas, had been to England and saw the success of railroads there. The cost of a canal and the number of locks necessary to get over the Allegheny Mountains was very high, and a railroad would not only provide better results, it would be much cheaper to build.

Events occurring in England influenced the decision-making process, among them the successful operation of a railroad between the English cities of Stockton and Darlington in 1825. The steam engine and railway cars had been supplied by George Stephenson, who named his engine the Locomotion, which gave rise to the term locomotive. Stephenson, assisted by his son, later won a race in 1829 held to determine the winning bidder to supply locomotives for another English railroad company. Stephenson named his winning locomotive the Rocket, and it was the first manmade land vehicle that could outrun a horse. The Rocket became famous and sparked the building of railroads in the United States, with the Baltimore & Ohio (soon known as the B&O) in the lead.

The Baltimore & Ohio also was noted for its use of the Tom Thumb, the steam locomotive designed by Peter Cooper in 1829 and built in the United States. Some early railroad companies tried to import locomotives from England, but they were too heavy for use on American tracks. The Tom Thumb was really an experimental engine, and in 1831 the B&O offered a $4,000 prize for a better locomotive. Phineas Davis of York, Pennsylvania, who called his creation the York, won the prize. By 1835 the B&O had seven operating locomotives, and obtaining suitable locomotives from American companies was no longer a problem.

The railroad spread rapidly throughout the eastern United States. From 23 miles of operating track mileage in 1830, the number jumped to 2,302 by the end of the decade, and reached 9,021 by 1850. It would ultimately grow to a peak of 254,036 in 1916, as railroads literally covered the United States.

July 7, 1838 — An act was passed designating all railroads in the United States as post routes. This was official recognition of the fact that railroads were far superior to regular roads for carrying the mail in any sort of weather. It was also recognition of the fact that railroads would eventually connect the majority of towns in the nation. After the act was passed, mail service by railroad increased rapidly.

The idea of sorting mail on trains instead of in the distributing post office soon evolved. Mail was sorted on the train for not only the post offices along the way; it was also sorted for distribution to the railroad branches that connected to the rail line on which the mail was being sorted. By 1930, more than 10,000 trains were used to move the mail into every city, town, and village in the United States. The use of the railroads by the post office grew as the railroads grew, and it fell as the importance of railroads fell. By 1965, only 190 trains carried mail, and, after the use of railroads to carry first-class mail fell nearly to zero in 1971, the last car to serve as a railway post office, one running between New York and Washington, D.C., made its final run on June 30, 1977. The railroads carried mail for about 140 years, essentially matching the time that railroads were considered an important part of American life.

August 13, 1859 — On this summer day in Council Bluffs, Iowa, a Republican candidate for President in next year's election, Abraham Lincoln, came to town to make a speech. He was well received, being from the neighboring state of Illinois, whose citizens had many interests similar to those of the citizens of Iowa. In the history of the railroads, the major event that took place on this day was a meeting between Lincoln and Glenville Dodge, a railroad engineer held to be at the top of his profession, even though he was only 28 years old at the time.

Lincoln had been a supporter of—and a lawyer for—the railroads for a long time. The Illinois Central Railroad had grown to be the longest railroad in the world in the early 1850s. Both as a member of the Illinois legislature, and as a lawyer for the railroad, Lincoln had supported its growth as well as the hotly debated practice of giving governmental land grants to help fund the railroad's construction. Railroads were seen as a driver of growth in the country, and the government land grants provided a good means of giving rights-of-way to the railroads while greatly improving the worth of the land held back by the government. Much land was given to the railroads, but the land's location made it nearly useless until the railroad arrived. Further, as the population boomed in the country (surpassing the population of Great Britain when it hit 23 million in 1850), mostly in the East, gold was being discovered in California, creating concern that foreign governments were enviously eyeing the vast open spaces of the United States with thoughts of political or armed conquest.

Lincoln was very much in favor of a transcontinental railroad to tie the states together from the Atlantic to the Pacific. The subject had been discussed for three decades, and in 1853 Congress had called for a survey of possible routes. Jefferson Davis, who was then secretary of war, sent out four teams of surveyors to explore alternatives from the Mexican border to the Canadian border. They did an excellent job, and eventually a railroad would be built along each route they surveyed. But not the first transcontinental line.

The slavery issue was the big obstacle to choosing a route. The southern states wanted the southern route so that slavery would be permitted in the states eventually joining the union along that route, while the northern states wanted a northern route for the opposite reason. Neither side would budge, and there was talk of the southern states seceding from the union if a Republican, such as Lincoln, who was opposed to slavery, were elected president the following year in 1860.

Lincoln wanted to talk to Dodge about a suitable route west, because Dodge had done considerable surveying west of the Missouri River to find just such a route. Dodge said that the best route was along the 42nd parallel, near their location at the time. Just across the Missouri River from Council Bluffs was Omaha, Nebraska, where the Platte River met the Missouri. The 42nd parallel essentially ran up the Platte River valley, which had a very slow grade upwards all the way to the Rocky Mountains. A railway through the Rocky Mountains along this route would descend to San Francisco on the other side. Council Bluffs was already connected with railroads running back to Chicago. Thus, the 42nd parallel should be chosen as the route for the transcontinental railroad. Lincoln agreed, and that route was chosen when he became president. The construction of the railroad was to be funded by land grants.

April 12, 1861— About one month after Lincoln was inaugurated as president, following his winning campaign in November of 1860, the Confederacy fired on Fort Sumter and the Civil War was underway. It would prove to be an especially bloody war (in which railroads for the first time would be used in the movement of troops and supplies), and the fate of the nation truly hung in the balance.

But ironically, one result of the war was that the southern states were no longer a part of Congress. While Lincoln was mostly involved in holding the country together on a north and south basis, and Glenville Dodge had joined the army of the North, neither forgot about the desire to join the country from east to west. Now there was no southern congressional opposition to a railroad along the 42nd parallel. Further, a national telegraph line from Missouri to San Francisco had been approved by Congress and would be completed in 1861. On June 28, 1861, the Central Pacific Railroad of California was incorporated with Leland Stanford, soon to be the Republican governor of California, as president, and with other prominent Californians such as Charles Crocker, Collis Huntington and Mark Hopkins as partners. The new railroad, under chief engineer Judah Benjamin, was determined to get over the Sierra Nevada mountains in California and head east.

On July 1, 1862, President Lincoln signed a bill, passed after much bickering by the Senate and the House, called the Pacific Railroad Bill. It created a corporation, called the Union Pacific Railroad, to build the railroad west from the Missouri River, while the Central Pacific Railroad would build east from Sacramento. Both railroads would be funded by land grants and government-guaranteed bonds. The railroads would have to complete their work by July 1, 1876, on pain of forfeiture. The bill was immensely complicated and would have to be substantially rewritten two years later. But one thing was clear. The bill contained elements of a race, and whoever built the most would get the most. The line was completed by May of 1869, more than seven years early and in half the time allotted. The race officially began on July 1, 1862, while the Civil War still raged.

November 30, 1867— The first train went through the Summit Tunnel of the Central Pacific Railroad. The Summit Tunnel was the last of 12 to be blasted through the Sierra Nevadas, and when a train finally passed through it marked the conquering of the mountain range, more than five years after the transcontinental railroad race had begun. The two sides began laying track towards each other as quickly as possible. The country was fascinated with the race to build the railroad, and many newspapers carried daily reports of the progress. In a way it helped to turn the country's attention away from the assassination of President Lincoln on April 14, 1865, only five days after the end of the Civil War. He had lived to see the end of the war, but not to help in the reconstruction of the nation nor to see the realization of his dream of a transcontinental railroad.

After the Civil War, many men from both sides came to work on the construction of the Union Pacific Railroad, the biggest thing then taking place in the nation. Many credited their ability to take orders and work as a team, learned during the Civil War, with their success on the railroad. The work force on the Union Pacific swelled to 10,000 men, many of them Irish-Americans. Similarly, the Central Pacific workforce grew as large as 10,000 men, with as many as 80 percent of them being Chinese immigrants.

The Central Pacific had a unique problem when they started work in earnest on the Sierra Nevada part of the route. Many of their workers came to work only long enough to get a new stake, and then took off into the mountains to look for gold. Sometimes only one week of hard work was enough for them to get together enough money to try mining again. As the railroad climbed higher into the Sierras, the men used the train as free transportation in their efforts to reach Nevada, where new silver strikes were being made. The turnover in the workforce was unmanageable.

In desperation, the railroad turned to the Chinese, who suffered severe discrimination in California, and who were considered to be too slight in stature to do the work. But the Chinese were the perfect solution. They worked well in groups, cooked their own more healthful food, thus missing fewer days off, and they saw the pay as a way to eventually live as emperors in their homeland (or to ultimately invest in their own businesses in the United States). The Chinese built the hardest part of the railroad through the Sierra Nevadas, and they were largely responsible for completing the dreamed-of railroad linking the nation east-to-west.

The Union Pacific had its own troubles, with Indian attacks on the Great Plains, and bad weather as they slogged through the then wild lands of Nebraska, Wyoming and Utah, racing against the Central Pacific, which had pushed into the relatively easy lands of Nevada after leaving California behind. As hard as their men were working in the field, both companies were working hard in Washington, D.C., trying to squeeze every dollar and political advantage possible out of a Congress more than willing to stick some of the company profits into its own pockets. The completion of the great undertaking would be followed by a scandal just as great.

July 26, 1868— A meeting was held at Fort Sanders, Wyoming, that included General Ulysses S. Grant, then preparing for the fall election that would make him president of the United States. Generals Sherman and Sheridan were also there, as was now ex-general Glenville Dodge, who was chief engineer of the Union Pacific Railroad, having left the Union Army at the end of the Civil War to assume the post. The key issue at the meeting was the interference Dodge felt he was getting from William "Doc" Durant, the nominal vice president of the Union Pacific, who was based in New York. Durant had been running the Union Pacific since it was formed, even though he only had the title of vice-president. He was a medical doctor, but he never practiced, and his true expertise was in doctoring railroad deals. Frankly, Durant's main interest was in stealing as much money as possible before the line was complete. Durant's basic plan was to build the line as shoddily as possible, keeping it going while he grabbed as much money as he could. (It must be said that the priority in railroad building at the time was to lay track as fast as possible so that the line could begin operation. Needed improvements could then come from operating revenues rather than further loans.)

The result of the meeting was that Dodge was backed by the powers-that-be, and Durant was told to quit interfering. Dodge was the clear victor, but Durant managed to keep his finger in the pie until the end. Durant symbolizes the worst of the excesses performed by the men who ran the Union Pacific (which was essentially bankrupt at the end of building the transcontinental line, but which survived to become number one in the railroad business, such as it was, at the end of the 20th century). Still, much of the credit for getting the project completed so far ahead of time has to go to Durant. Similarly, many consider the original members of the Central Pacific Railroad to be robber barons, but they risked their own money to get the line running, and they built their part of the transcontinental line at dazzling speed.

There was a lot of money made by lots of people in the building of the transcontinental line, but it was so successful and led to such growth in the United States that most of the related scandals uncovered later were, to a large extent, brushed aside by the country as a whole.

May 10, 1869— The date on which the famous "golden spike" was hammered home and the transcontinental railroad was declared complete. The ceremony was originally scheduled for Saturday, May 8, but the Union Pacific train bringing its delegates to the designated meeting point at Promontory Summit, Utah, was delayed because heavy rains had damaged a bridge along the route. So the train bearing Leland Sanford, special guests of the Central Pacific line, and the actual golden spike had to sit and wait two days for the Union Pacific to arrive.

The assembled officials argued for an hour about protocol even as the

ceremony was about to begin at last, at noon on Monday, May 10. A laurel
tie was brought forward, together with a silver hammer and the golden spike.
There was a predrilled hole for the spike so only a tap would be needed to
drive it. Durant of the Union Pacific and Sanford of the Central Pacific were
to alternately drive in the spike, the solution to the long argument as to who
would have the honor of doing so. Durant hit the spike, but Stanford some-
how missed and hit the rail. No matter. The telegraph operators were set to
signal the world as soon as Sanford was done, and so they did. The wire
"DONE!" was sent out. Bells pealed across the nation, including the Lib-
erty Bell in Philadelphia. Parades began, among them Chicago's biggest of
the century. After the two trains ceremoniously rode over the point of junc-
ture and then backed up, the transcontinental railroad was a reality — seven
years ahead of schedule.

The nation — and the world — had been fascinated by the details of the
race, as carried every day in the newspapers. The competitiveness of the race
had led the lines to make some poor — and expensive — decisions in the drive
to be first. For hundreds of miles the two lines had been grading land for
future tracks in full sight of each other, one line going west and the other
going east. The Central Pacific played the better game of politics, and although
the lines "met" at Promontory Summit in Utah, the Central Pacific legally
owned the right-of-way about 50 miles further east and the Union Pacific
had to sell their completed track to the Central Pacific.

There were other battles, and often they were purely competitive rather
than mule-headed. One such battle involving speed took place when the
Union Pacific laid eight miles of track in one day, on October 26, 1868, then
a world's record. The average was just over two miles a day. The Central
Pacific bided its time until about six months later on April 27, 1869. The Union
Pacific had only nine miles to go to the meeting point, while the Central
Pacific had about fourteen miles to go. On that day the Central Pacific
announced that they were going to build ten miles of track in one day to
break the record. If they succeeded, the Union Pacific would not have enough
room left to set a new record in turn.

On April 28 the Central Pacific workers, who were following a proce-
dure for laying track quickly that was worked out in secret by their bosses,
began the task of building the rail line before a crowd that included a wagon
loaded with Union Pacific officials, who had come to jeer and laugh at what
they were sure would be the humiliation of the Central Pacific. They started
at sunrise, at 7:15, and by lunchtime at 1:30 P.M., the Central Pacific workers had laid six miles of track. An Army officer who was watching said the
men moved at the pace of a marching army with a ribbon of track following in their wake. After a leisurely lunch of one hour, work slowed in the
afternoon because they had to bend track to fit curves on the railroad, but
by 7 P.M. they had laid ten miles and fifty-six feet of track.

At least one Union Pacific field boss wanted to tear up some of the track his workers had already lain to give them enough room to take the record back. But enough was enough. The Central Pacific workers had their new record (it has never been broken), and it was time to stop the race now that the culmination of the whole process was less than two weeks away. The huge work forces that had grown to 10,000 men on each side began to melt away, and only a relatively few who were working on finishing touches took part in the final ceremonies. Many of the workers went on to build other lines, even transcontinental lines along the other routes initially surveyed starting in 1853, but no other rail lines would have the impact of the first transcontinental line. Track mileage would continue to grow in the country until it reached its peak almost 50 years later. Railroads would dominate transportation to a degree undreamed of even in the glow of the completion of the first transcontinental line, only to begin a slow decline into near-irrelevance.

September 4, 1872— *The New York Times* ran a gigantic headline about what they called "The King of Frauds." The story described in great detail the many devious practices — real or imagined — involved in the building of the transcontinental railroad. Members of Congress were accused of lining their pockets with gifts of stock and cash from both sides, and hearings were held that lasted for about six months.

The hearings were as popular in the newspapers as the actual building of the railroad itself had once been. Congress did finally issue some declarations of censure, but ironically one of the most culpable people—"Doc" Durant—was gone, having been forced off the Union Pacific Board of Directors by word from President Grant, just after the completion of the line in May of 1869. This had resulted from the meeting (described above) on July 26, 1868. It was ironic that Durant escaped censure, but he finally lost all of his ill-gotten gains in the panic of 1873, and he died a forgotten man, on October 5, 1885.

Continuing controversy has followed in the wake of the 1872-73 hearings, much of it focusing on whether the federal government got its money's worth out of the bonds and land grants used to build the transcontinental railroad. Historian Steven Ambrose wrote an excellent book in 2000 on the building of the transcontinental railroad, but hesitated to undertake the project because he had always been taught — and believed — that the men who built the railroads were great villains. He pointed out that the government finally made out very well on its investment, and concluded that "An automatic reaction that big business is always on the wrong side, corrupt and untrustworthy, is too easy, and the error is compounded if we fail to distinguish between incentives, for example, and fraud."

In spite of some errors along the way, the transcontinental railroad was the greatest investment in improved transportation that the government made before 1900, achieving the public good and making a good return in the process. Railroads covered the country after the transcontinental railroad was complete, growing from 30,626 miles of track in 1860 to 193,346 in 1900.

August 4, 1877 — Nikolaus Otto, a German inventor, was granted a patent for his design of a four-cylinder internal combustion gas motor, which he then later licensed to be built for sale in the United States. Otto had previously received a patent on April 21, 1866, in Germany for a two-stroke engine, and along with many other inventors had been working since then to improve the operation of such engines. An improved engine of this type was exhibited at the great Centennial Exposition in Philadelphia in 1876 (and probably seen by Henry Ford's father, who was in attendance). Using the basic concept of other inventors, Otto was the first to build a working four-cycle engine and thus was the first to patent it. The engine was called the "silent Otto" because it was much quieter than the previous design. It was also much more efficient. When the "silent Otto" was shown at the Paris Exhibition of 1878, it was obvious that it was the culmination of all the work done in the previous 20 years or so to develop internal combustion engines. It swept away all competitors, just as predicted at the time.

Otto's engine marked the impending demise of the steam engine. Just as the steam engine had represented the beginning of the Industrial Revolution and the railroads, the internal combustion engine led to the automobile and the airplane, the next revolution in transportation. Ironically, just as the railroads were reaching their peak in power and influence, the invention that would cause their decline was being rapidly improved and spreading throughout the world. Just as the railroad arrived near the peak of canal building and quickly wiped out the canals, the internal combustion engine arrived on the scene and the decline of the railroads began. It would happen slowly, while the internal combustion engine proved its worth in automobiles and airplanes, but the decline of railroads was inevitable from this day.

October 27, 1879 — Thomas A. Edison developed the first electric light bulb. This development was significant to transportation because Edison also developed the infrastructure to utilize his invention. Edison realized he couldn't just sell light bulbs; he had to make it possible for people to use them. He thus developed a complete electrical distribution system, including generators, motors, light sockets, junction boxes, safety fuses, underground conductors, and related devices to build power plants to supply his new light bulb.

The immediate result of this effort was the famous Pearl Street plant built in New York City during 1881 and 1882. It was the first central power plant built in the world. The long-term result of his work was the creation of the electric power industry. Streetcars using electricity as their power source soon began to appear in many cities, as described below. Henry Ford had a job as foreman at the company providing electrical power to Detroit when he first began to tinker with horseless carriages. Ford was very good at his job and his supervisors tended to leave him on his own, which gave him lots of time to experiment. Later, Ford and Edison became very close friends, due to their mutual admiration of each other's work and work ethic.

November 18, 1883— At noontime on this Sunday in November, a suggestion of how to coordinate time on all railroads went into effect. The nation was divided into four time zones, and noontime, for example, would be at the same time throughout each individual time zone. The time zones would be fixed at one hour behind the previous zone as one traveled from east to west. This plan enabled the many railroads across the country to have consistent schedules, and was quickly adopted by the nation as a whole. "Railroad time" became standard everywhere. Before this agreement each railroad measured its own time, using a sundial each had wherever its headquarters happened to be.

It is hard to believe such an obvious (in hindsight) solution had been in discussion formally for 11 years, ever since a meeting among train officials was held in St. Louis in 1872 to address the issue. The process became law during World War I, when the government recognized the obvious and made time zones official by passing the Standard Time Act, in March of 1918.

Railroads were so much a part of everyone's life in 1883 that there was no resistance to adopting such a commonsense railroad practice on a national basis. Still, great opposition was growing to the perceived arrogance of the railroads and their monopoly on the nation's transportation. Farmers were especially vocal in their criticism of the railroads. Rates were set by the railroads essentially on the basis of what the traffic would bear. In small towns, which is where many farmers lived, there was usually only one railroad and rates were high. In bigger towns and cities, where there was much competition among railroads, rates were lower. A customer shipping long distance through many cities would get the benefit of relatively lower rates. A farmer trying to reach a market in a nearby big city had to pay high rates to ship his product from a local community with only one railroad available. Many of these farmers had mortgaged their farms to buy stock that promoters had insisted the communities must buy to attract a railroad to their community. The stock usually lost much of its value, because the railroad barons back East issued piles of stock to support their ambitious plans to expand and merge their railroads.

In 1867, on December 4, Oliver Kelley, a Bostonian by birth working in the Washington, D.C. post office, founded an association called the National

Grange of the Patrons of Husbandry, commonly called the Grange. Kelley was essentially an activist who had been shocked by the poverty of southern farmers he had seen on a trip through the region. Kelley's movement to better the lot of farmers through combined action spread like wildfire when he took his cause to the Midwest. By 1875, 20,000 chapters of the Grange had been organized, and the movement was becoming a political force. State governments took notice and began to threaten rules and regulations to control the actions of the railroads, to benefit the public. As the 1880s dawned, Congress was getting ready to consider this issue as well.

The attitude of the railroads at this time was best expressed by a comment made around 1883 by William H. Vanderbilt, son of the famous Commodore Vanderbilt whose huge fortune included the New York Central Railroad, which he had left to his son William. In the middle of a fare war with the mighty Pennsylvania Railroad for passengers going to Chicago, a reporter asked a question about running the railroad for the benefit of the public. Vanderbilt responded succinctly, "The public be damned!" The public viewed it as a declaration of war by the railroads, and despite all of their power it was a war the railroads would lose.

February 4, 1887 — An act was passed creating the Interstate Commerce Commission (ICC). This was the response of Congress to the political pressure being brought by the Grange and its supporters. The ICC was ineffective at first, as the act was poorly written, partly because Congress was still uncomfortable with the idea of interfering with private enterprise in a capitalistic society. Some unfavorable Supreme Court rulings also hindered the ICC from becoming an effective regulator.

However, the camel had its nose under the tent. In the trust-busting atmosphere of the Roosevelt administration at the turn of the century, and with some changes in the law and some favorable Supreme Court rulings, by 1906 the ICC was a formidable opponent of the railroads' many abuses. For the rest of its existence, the ICC (which expired by the end of the 20th century) would play a large part in the long decline of the railroads, even though it finally tried to help them in the end.

February 2, 1888 — Frank J. Sprague successfully ran streetcars powered by electricity over his electrified test system in Richmond, Virginia. Sprague was born on July 25, 1857, and had graduated from the U.S. Naval Academy in 1874. He was always interested in things electrical, and while on duty with the Navy he had visited the London subway in 1882. It was the first subway in the world, but Sprague thought the smoke spewed out by the steam locomotive pulling the subway cars was intolerable, and he thought that electric propulsion would be much better if it could be developed.

After leaving the Navy, in 1883, Sprague went to work for Thomas A. Edison at Edison's famous Menlo Park Laboratories in New Jersey. Edison had built an experimental locomotive driven by electricity in 1880, following the 1879 example of Werner Siemens of Berlin (German and French scientists had developed electric motors in the mid–1800s, and Siemens had begun manufacturing alternators, which could produce alternating current — AC — from direct current — DC — around 1878). But Edison was much more interested in street lighting than transportation, so Sprague left Menlo Park to form his own company in 1884.

Sprague's company, the Sprague Electric Railway and Motor Company, had some early growing pains, but finally signed a contract in May 1887 that resulted in what is generally regarded as the world's first successful streetcar electrification system, in Richmond, Virginia. The streetcar electrification of the nation truly began with this test. Many other systems were in development at the time, but Sprague's was the first unqualified success.

Perhaps the most notable event related to Sprague's work in Richmond occurred in the summer of 1888. Officials from the Boston streetcar system, a huge system with 2,000 cars and 8,000 horses, came to visit. They, as did many others, wanted to eliminate the horses and horse manure from the downtown traffic of Boston. It was expected they would go with a cable system — of the sort still operating in San Francisco — as others were doing or proposing. They were impressed with Sprague's system, but decided against it because of concerns that it would be overloaded if a traffic jam put all of the cars on a line out on the road at once.

Sprague sprung into action. He had all the Richmond cars assembled together at night, after the line had ceased operating for the day. Then he roused the key officials out of bed in their hotel, and demonstrated that the line could operate with such a load. The Boston delegation then decided to replace its horse-drawn cars with electric cars. The Sprague system began operating in Boston within about six months, and within three years 200 streetcar systems had converted to electricity or were in the process of doing so. The growth produced by the Sprague system is perhaps best summarized by the fact that in 1890 the total street railway miles were below 8,000, and 75 percent of it was powered by animals. In 1902 there were 22,500 miles of track, and animals powered only one percent. Sprague is properly known as the key individual in the development of urban mass transportation, and he made a major contribution to rapid transit as well at the end of the century, as described in the entry for June 6, 1892.

January 8, 1889 — J.P. Morgan, first among equals in the world of finance, called a meeting of railroad titans in his sumptuous mansion in New York. The public was told that the attendees were going to discuss the issue of rates, over which there was much public concern. They had actually gathered to form a gentlemen's agreement to create a trust that would set rates, fending off rate wars that would reduce profits.

This meeting was typical of the actions of the railroad barons. Buy-outs and mergers concentrated the ownership of the nation's railroads into relatively few hands, hands that were anxious to profit from a monopoly position. In the East the New York Central and the Pennsylvania Railroad ruled by the end of the century. In the South, a small group of lines controlled by Morgan held sway. Edward H. Harriman controlled the Union Pacific, Southern Pacific, and Illinois Central to rule in the West. Jay Gould dominated the Southwest, and James Hill merged the Great Northern with the Northern Pacific. Other famous, or infamous, names like Daniel Drew and Jim Fisk rose to the top tier at times.

The railroad empires listed above accounted for about half of the over 200,000 miles of track in the United States shortly after the turn of the century. The ability of just these relatively few individuals to control the railroad business, by far the biggest single industry in the country, led to understandable abuses of the public interest. The railroad industry was ripe for a fall, and that's just what it did in the 20th century.

September 25, 1891 — Henry Ford moved into Detroit from his nearby Dearborn farm to take a job as an engineer at the Edison Illuminating Company. Ford, born on July 30, 1863, was now a 28-year-old married man and had always been interested in mechanical things. He had served as an apprentice in Detroit machine shops when he was only 16, and he had also developed his mechanical skill working as a watch repairer. When he returned to his father's farm after his stint in the Detroit machine shops he served as a manufacturer's representative for farm machinery companies, and established a reputation as someone who could fix nearly any kind of machinery.

Ford had been reading deeply about horseless carriages driven by the new gasoline motors, and he was determined to build one. He took the job at the Edison Company in part to learn what he felt he needed to know about electricity in order to proceed with his new business ideas. Ford rose to be chief engineer at the company, where he gained a high reputation for his ability to repair the company's various engines and generators. He was left mainly on his own, enabling him to continue his horseless carriage experiments. Around 1893 he established an "experimental room," where he could work while taking advantage of the tools and facilities available at the company. He also had a workshop at home. Ford was a little over three years away from the famous June 4, 1896 debut of his Quadricycle, but still a decade away from founding the Ford Motor Company.

June 6, 1892— The first elevated train opened in Chicago. The elevated trains were called the "L" in Chicago, and still are. In New York they were also called the "el," and eventually that designation became preferred on the East Coast. The elevated train is one form of "rapid" transit, while the subway is another. The distinction between "mass" transit and "rapid" transit is that rapid transit has its own right-of-way and is thus not subject to the traffic jams of regular transportation. However, rapid transit is limited to transportation along its right-of-way, just like the railroad. In fact, rapid transit is simply the adaptation of the railroad to operation in the middle of a city.

The very first el began running in New York in July of 1866. It used cable-drawn cars (like those still operating in San Francisco). Soon steam locomotives were used to power the cars along their elevated track. The smoke was objectionable, but by 1893 the el was carrying a half-million riders every day, which convinced Chicago to begin their own. Electrification came initially to the L in Chicago in 1895 and to the el in New York in 1896. In 1898 Sprague got in the act again (*see entry for* February 2, 1888) and developed a multiple-unit control system to use in electrifying any kind of train. Every electrified rapid transit system and electrified railway system in the world today uses a variation of Sprague's 1898 system.

December 15, 1892— It was during the closing month of 1892 that Orville and Wilbur Wright decided to open a bicycle shop in their hometown of Dayton, Ohio. Both brothers were self-taught mechanics, although neither officially graduated from high school, and they had previously been running a printing service in Dayton, and had made unsuccessful attempts to print a newspaper of their own. Wilbur was the older brother, born on April 16, 1867, while Orville was born on August 19, 1871. Orville had been the driving force in the printing business, deciding to extend a boyhood sideline into a full-time business rather than finishing high school. The brothers were very close, and Wilbur became part of the business, which they ran successfully for about three years before deciding to take up something else while a friend operated the printing business. That something else was the bicycle, which was becoming a national craze in the 1890s.

Civil War veteran Colonel Albert Pope was the national guru of bicycles. A Hartford, Connecticut, manufacturer and marketer, in 1878 Pope arranged to have the Weed Sewing Machine Company of Hartford build an American-made version of the "ordinary" bicycle from England, the kind with a high front wheel. Within a decade, Pope produced about a quarter-million of the bikes. Then in 1887, Pope introduced, again from England, the so-called safety bike. This bike had two wheels of equal size with a chain-drive transmission system in a sturdy frame. It was easier to ride than the ordinary, and it was claimed that its modified V frame made the bicycle the ultimate in exercise for females. The bike caught on, and at the peak of the 1890s craze, there were over 300 companies producing over a million bicycles per year.

Both brothers bought bikes, and Orville performed well in some local races. They decided to go into the bicycle business, and their shop was opened at the end of 1892. They were quite successful, in spite of much local competition, because the Wrights offered repair services, bike assembly from pre-ordered parts, and completely custom bikes built within their shop. The Wrights were true artisans in a world rapidly turning to the techniques of mass-production. They soon had to move to a larger store, then they moved again to a place large enough to contain both their bicycle business and their printing business. By 1896 they had moved everything again to another larger building, and now that they were successful bicycle builders, they once again began to look for new worlds to conquer.

November 28, 1895 — This was the date finally set for the Chicago-Evanston race sponsored by the *Chicago Times Herald*. Over a rough course in cold weather, a car driven (and built) by Frank Duryea finished first. The Duryea brothers, Charles and Frank, of Springfield, Massachusetts, had been building a horseless carriage since 1890. The idea and original plans were Charles's, but as he was involved in a bicycle business in Peoria, Illinois, much of the actual work fell on Frank's shoulders. At the end of the summer of 1893, Frank had the car running, and the brothers have a credible claim to being the builders of the first American gasoline automobile. Frank Duryea continued to make more improvements in the car, and the improved design was entered in the 1895 race.

The results of the race triggered a great burst of activity by several inventors who were building experimental cars. The Duryeas immediately formed a production company, and began to offer cars for sale in February of 1896. They produced a baker's dozen of cars and won some more racing prizes, but they did not stay long on the American scene. Competitors were quickly appearing who would begin to sell thousands of cars.

June 4, 1896 — In the early hours of the morning, Henry Ford knocked down some bricks of the wall of the shed in his backyard, and managed to get his experimental car — later called a Quadricycle — out of the shed and onto the street. Henry Ford had built his first car.

He continued working on the car, not much more than a glorified motorized bicycle with extra seating, then finally sold it for $200 in the fall and began work on an improved model. Ford sold the car after returning from an August convention in New York, which he attended for his company, and at which he met and was encouraged in his efforts by Thomas Edison. Ford had not built the car for sale but as a vehicle for experimentation. However, he decided to accept an offer for the car so he would have the money to build a new and improved model. The Ford Motor Company was now only seven years away.

August 10, 1896 — While Henry Ford was attending the convention in New York and meeting and being encouraged by Thomas Edison, a man named Otto Lilienthal was dying in a hospital in Berlin. Lilienthal was known as the "Flying Man" for his many glider flights in Germany since 1889. On August 9, 1896, one of the flights had gone wrong and Lilienthal had fallen and broken his spine, and he died the next day. Lilienthal was a serious experimenter, and the Wright brothers had followed his exploits in the magazines and newspapers of the day.

The Wright brothers' interest in the field of human flight, which had been lying just below the surface, was strengthened by Lilienthal's death. They were not aware at the time that in the summer of the same year, on June 22, 1896, a civil engineer named Octave Canute traveled into the sand dunes of Indiana, near Chicago, to make some experimental flights with gliders. Canute had become more or less a one-man clearinghouse in the United States for news about things having to do with manned flight, and he had been successful enough in his career to be able to indulge his avocation of manned flight.

Nothing dramatic came out of Canute's flights in 1896, nor out of experiments made in the same year by Samuel Langley, secretary of the Smithsonian Institution in Washington, D.C., although Langley's work eventually triggered an invitation from the War Department to conduct some experiments in secret with their support. But the Wright brothers were getting involved with the question of human flight just at the time many inventors around the world were beginning to pursue the field in earnest. In just three years they would be deeply involved with the exploits of men like Canute and Langley, and their research that began in 1896 would eventually take them to a place called Kitty Hawk, North Carolina, to conduct glider experiments.

September 1, 1897 — The city of Boston became the first American city to construct a subway system, which began operation on this date. Ground had been broken on March 28, 1895. Because of political infighting, ground was not broken on the first true subway in New York City until May 24, 1900, and the subway did not open until October 27, 1904. However, the Boston subway was a "shallow" subway constructed just under city streets, built to avoid specific congested areas. The New York subway was a "deep-bore" or "tube" subway that ran in a deep tunnel and was powered by electricity. This kind of subway was not built by excavation, but by burrowing under city streets like a mole. The New York system grew to be 722 miles in length (the distance from New York to Chicago), and it was still the longest subway in the world into the 1990s.

A subway system of the length of the New York subway, with its almost 500 stations, is to a large extent not subject to the limitations imposed by the fact that true rapid transit systems can only go where their right-of-way permits them to go. As late as 1990, nearly half the workers in New York used the subway to get to work. However, the New York subway suffers from the same problem as nearly all mass transit and rapid transit systems in the United States — the fares are not sufficient to cover the cost of operation, largely due to high unionized labor costs. This has been an issue for most of the 20th century. Both the then-new Boston and New York systems were built as municipal systems in an attempt to avoid this problem, but it did not work out that way.

Although mass transit and rapid transit systems are important to the cities they serve, preventing massive traffic jams and transporting large numbers of people, in terms of the total transportation movement of goods, services, and people in the country, these local systems account for only a small percentage. Transit trips per capita fell from a peak of 178 just after World War II, to just over 35 in 1990. The non-war peak year was 1926 at 163, and the average today is barely higher than it was in 1890 (just over 32), before the subways were built. The automobile is responsible.

August 5, 1899 — The Detroit Automobile Company was formally organized. The mayor of Detroit was among a number of stockholders who put together a company to build automobiles utilizing the talents of Henry Ford. Ford had continued building experimental cars, and after some impressive demonstrations, others had decided to join the mayor, who was enthusiastic about Ford's capabilities. Henry Ford quit his job at the Edison Illuminating Company and committed himself to building cars full time.

Unfortunately Ford only built a few cars for the new company. He recognized that what he built was not competitive with what was available in the marketplace, and he wanted to continue improving the design. But the stockholders wanted to produce cars and earn some revenue. Ford, however, had decided to build a race car to gain some publicity and credibility in the market, and the Detroit Automobile Company was dissolved in November of 1900. But one of its stockholders agreed to back Ford in his new venture, and he set out to build a racing car. The venture would be a great success. The Ford Motor Company was now only two years away.

August 24, 1899—Wilbur Wright wrote a letter to the Weather Bureau in Washington, D.C. In reply to his request for information on wind velocities in the vicinity of Chicago, the Weather Bureau sent him data on the average winds in August and September at all weather stations in the United States. This was the second important letter Wilbur wrote in 1899 regarding human flight, a subject in which both brothers were now deeply involved.

On May 30, 1899, Wilbur had written to the Smithsonian asking for general information about the subject. The response included a number of reprints and some book suggestions, and the Wright brothers entered the worlds, among others, of Otto Lilienthal, Samuel Langley, and Octave Canute (*see entry for* August 10, 1896). They ordered the suggested books immediately, and began their careful, methodical study of the subject of human flight.

The Wright brothers' methodical approach to their new field of interest was important. They quickly decided they were not interested in lighter-than-air flight (flight by means of balloons). They divided past experiments into attempted powered flights and glider flights. After some study they concluded that the trick was to learn how to control glider flights. Once that big step had been accomplished, adding a source of power should be comparatively simple. The brothers built a biplane (two wings) with a five-foot wingspan to be flown as a kite to collect data on the control of flight. As a result, they learned how to produce lateral control by using wing warping, a twisting and bending of the wings that the brothers had observed in the flight of pigeons. They were convinced that they had learned enough to take the next step, which was to experiment with a man-carrying glider. They calculated from their reading that they needed stronger winds than those available near their hometown of Dayton; hence the letter to the Weather Bureau.

On May 13, 1900, Wilbur wrote to Oliver Canute, asking for specific advice on a location to experiment with their manned glider flights. Wilbur added that the demands of his business required that he experiment between September and January. Considering his Indiana dunes unsuitable so late in the year, Canute did not suggest them, but said that a sandy place was best for the crash landings the experimenters could expect, and for good weather at the right in the time he recommended San Diego or Pine Island, Florida. Canute also said that the coasts of South Carolina or Georgia might offer suitable places. Wilbur re-studied his data from the Weather Bureau, and found that Kitty Hawk, North Carolina, offered sea breezes of the strength needed, and was closer to Dayton than any of the places Canute suggested.

Wilbur wrote again to the weather station at Kitty Hawk on August 3, 1900, requesting information about accommodations on what was essentially a narrow strip of sand off the North Carolina mainland. He received friendly replies from the weather bureau and the husband of the local postmistress. Tents would be necessary for housing, but the people were friendly and hospitable in all other respects.

So it was that in the fall of 1900 the Wright brothers set off for Kitty Hawk to begin assembling and testing the newly designed glider. They spent the falls of 1900, 1901, and 1902 in Kitty Hawk, gaining the knowledge they needed to build a glider suitable for powered flight, which they would test in 1903. They had much to learn in those three years, but they would take the same methodical approach they had used so far, and they would ultimately succeed in their quest for manned flight.

November 30, 1901— The dissolved Detroit Automobile Company (*see entry for* August 5, 1899) came back to life on this date. It was reorganized under the new name of the Henry Ford Company (the Ford Motor Company was still 18 months in the future). This was a direct result of Henry Ford's victory in an auto race with the famous Alexander Winton the previous month. The publicity and credibility that Ford and his backer, William H. Murphy, had said would come from successful racing had come true, at least for them.

Ford was listed as the engineer for the new company, and was credited with 1,000 shares of stock, worth $10,000, although he paid nothing into the company. Ford ultimately felt he was not being given enough compared to his value to the company. Further, he felt that the others in the company wanted to focus on a commercial car for which they could charge the most money, while he was still thinking of a cheap car, produced in quantity, that would be affordable to a large number of people.

As a result Henry Ford left his new company on March 10, 1902, a little over three months after it had been formed. With the backing of Tom Cooper, a former bicycle racer who was involved in Ford's racing victory, he was determined to build another racer that would be the fastest car in the world, capable of averaging 60 miles per hour, or in the parlance of the time, "a mile a minute."

One of the new cars, both of which had four-cylinder engines, was called "999" in honor of a famous train from the New York Central railroad. The train made a run from New York to Chicago in 1893, breaking 100 miles per hour with a record of 112.5 miles per hour near Batavia, New York. An old friend of Cooper's, Barney Oldfield, also an ex–bicycle racer, was selected to drive the car. Oldfield won the rematch with Alexander Winton and two others on October 25, 1902, winning a prize of $1,000 as well as great fame. Oldfield set a new American record of five minutes and twenty-eight seconds for five miles, an average of less than one minute and six seconds per mile. Oldfield later set new records for the five-mile distance, and only a few months after the race he ran a mile in only one and a fifth seconds over the one-minute target. Oldfield became famous as "a mile-a-minute" Oldfield, and Henry Ford's stature in the automotive world grew even higher. Ford and Cooper's relationship cooled, and Ford sold him the racers. It was Ford's third failure in business, but a new and greater company was about to be born.

After Henry Ford left, the backers of the Henry Ford Company arranged for the business to be taken over by Henry M. Leland, a well-known veteran owner of a celebrated machine shop and a familiar face on the Detroit automobile scene. Leland used the basic design for the "commercial car" Henry Ford had created, put in a one-cylinder engine of his own design, and called the company the Cadillac Automobile Company. It developed a reputation for high quality and reliability. The cars sold well and became one of the key components of the General Motors corporation that was organized in 1908. The Cadillac brand, of course, still exists today, but few know that it started out life as a Ford.

October 28, 1902 — The Wright brothers broke camp at Kitty Hawk, North Carolina. They had conducted between 700 and 1,000 glider flights during their 1902 tests and were quite pleased with the results. This was the third consecutive year of experimenting, and they expected to try more experimental flights in 1903, but they soon raised their ambitions.

After reviewing their results to date, and talking to their friend Octave Canute, they decided they had accumulated enough data on flight control to try a powered flight. They tried to patent their three-axis control system the following year, but the patent was rejected on the grounds that it was too vague. The patent office recommended that they avail themselves of the services of a professional patent attorney, which they ultimately did in 1904, starting out all over again. It was the first of many mistakes they would make in the process of getting and protecting their patents.

But they were right in believing that they knew enough about flight control to move on to powered flight. They spent the first part of 1903 redesigning their glider to take on the added weight of an engine and propellers. They also turned their hand to designing a lightweight internal combustion motor and a pair of high-efficiency propellers. Over the years they had created an extensive airplane workshop, including a small wind tunnel, and they had the tools they needed as well as considerable reference data, so they were well equipped to take on these new tasks in their careful, methodical way. In their view, 1903 was to be the year they achieved powered flight, and so it was.

June 16, 1903 — The Ford Motor Company was officially incorporated. A total of 1,000 shares of stock were issued, of which Henry Ford and his main investor, coal distributor Alexander Malcomson, received 255 shares each, or a combined 51 percent of the total. Ten other investors held the other 490 shares. Banker John Gray, also involved in the Malcomson coal business, held 105 shares, while none of the other investors held more than 50 shares. Each of the Dodge brothers, who had advanced the company considerable sums in material, held 50 shares each, but they were so combative that their shares hardly counted as a voting bloc. Henry Ford, as a major stockholder, finally felt that he was being properly rewarded for his talents and contribution to a company. As a result he was fully involved, working for the success of the company as a whole rather than working on side projects, as he had in his previous three business attempts.

The beginning of the company actually dated back to August 16, 1902, when Henry Ford was supposedly working with Tom Cooper to build racers (*see entry for* November 30, 1901). Ford went to his friend Malcomson on that date, seeking backing to build a new car on "novel" principles that was sure to be a success. After the race results proved him right two months later, Ford was a hot property, but he stuck to his agreement with Malcomson. More money was made available and Ford and his key employees worked hard on the new car. In November, Ford and Malcomson strengthened their agreement. Ford understood that he would be a major stockholder if the company succeeded, and he worked that much harder.

But success seemed far off, and the company was approaching a cash flow crisis in July, in spite of the fact that the Dodge brothers had taken stock in payment for their supplies and the other stockholders had paid in cash. There were 650 cars (called the Model A) built, but no buyers. On July 15, 1903, a Dr. E. Pfennig sent in a check for $850, and the cash flow crisis was quickly resolved as orders began to pour in to the new company. Many analysts made much of the fact that the first purchase was made by a doctor, and credit doctors buying cars to make their rounds for a large part of the sales in those early years. That may well have been, but several decades later it was discovered that Dr. Pfenning was a dentist.

The Ford Motor Company flourished, declaring dividends that paid off their investors within one year, while still leaving them holding shares in a very promising company. However, the big question of the day for many automobile companies of the time — whether to aim at the high-priced part of the market or the lower-priced part and make less profit per car but more total profits in higher volume — soon became a major issue at the Ford Motor Company.

December 17, 1903— The Wright brothers (with Orville doing the flying) made the first powered airplane flight. It was the culmination of four years of testing at Kitty Hawk, not to mention the time spent in their workshop and in their study of the problem. The 1903 session was conducted in poor weather, and some twisted shafts had to be sent to Dayton for repair, while the Wright brothers waited anxiously for their return in time to run the final test before the weather became too poor for experimenting.

Finally, on Thursday the 17th, they had made all their repairs and there was sufficient wind. Before a few witnesses from a nearby lifeguard station, Orville (it was his turn to fly as determined by a coin toss), became the first human to make a powered flight. The flight lasted only about 12 seconds, and he flew only about 120 feet, but as he said later, it was "The first in the history of the world in which a machine carrying a man had raised itself by its own power into the air in full flight, had sailed forward without reduction of speed, and had finally landed at a point as high as that from which it started."

Wilbur made the fourth and best flight of the day, covering 852 feet in 59 seconds before a movement of the rudder control caused a soft crash. However, while pictures were being taken of the Flyer, as the brothers had optimistically named their machine, the wind turned it over several times and the damage precluded any more flights. Still, the brothers had accomplished their goal and were satisfied to break camp and be home by Christmas, as they had promised the family back in Dayton. Orville sent a brief telegram about their success, and a careful, methodical publicity campaign was set in motion. The brothers wanted the world to know they had succeeded, but they did not want too much information to become known until they had received their patent. It was the first of many mistakes the brothers would make in the next decade that would somewhat tarnish their image as pioneers in flight.

Their flight did not result in instant fame. Many papers confused the news of the Wright brothers' flight with the disastrous attempt at flight made by Samuel P. Langley nine days before, on December 8, 1903. His "Aerodrome" crashed into the Potomac River immediately after launch, and not for the first time, before a jeering horde of reporters who had sniffed out the supposedly secret work that Langley was doing for the U.S. Government. Other newspapers thought that the Langley attempt had proved once again that human flight was a long way in the future, and treated the news of a supposedly successful attempt in the boondocks of North Carolina as the work of crackpots. The relative secrecy in which the brothers wished to work did not help matters.

The Wright brothers decided to focus all their efforts on the next step in the progress of the flying machine. With money in the bank, they eased their way out of the bicycle business and turned full time to improving the Flyer. They mistakenly believed that they were many years ahead of the competition, and that they could easily attract government interest in their invention. Although many things did not work out as they planned, they kept improving the Flyer and testing it in a field near Dayton (local winds now being no issue), and in the late summer and fall of 1908 they burst upon the world scene, demonstrating their newest version of the Flyer before the eyes of an astonished and adoring public in both France and the United States. They achieved both fame and fortune, but it still did not work out quite as planned.

January 9, 1904— Just as the Wright brothers were relaxing at home after their little-noticed historic flight the month before (see previous entry), Henry Ford was becoming enmeshed in an argument about the direction his new company should take. On this day he went out on frozen Lake St. Clair, just outside Detroit, hoping to set a new speed record and gain more publicity for Ford cars.

Ford succeeded, and his cars were a success in 1904. The Ford Motor Company was now offering Models B, C, and F. Each was better than the initial Model A offered for sale, and the more expensive Model B was promoted by Ford's speed records. But the Models C and F were more in line with the cheaper cars he wanted to build. Their sales outstripped those of the Model B. The arguments over the type of car to build were soon to come to a head.

November 22, 1905— The Ford Manufacturing Company was formed. The intent of the company was to supply engines and gears to the Ford Motor Company. These parts would be used in the manufacture of the Model N, the new cheap car that would replace the Models C and F in the new lineup for the Ford Motor Company, while keeping the profits earned on these parts, now supplied by the Dodge Brothers, within the Manufacturing Company. An additional unstated motive was to push Malcomson aside. He had no stock in the new company, and Henry Ford considered him not only of no use in the Ford Motor Company, but actually a hindrance because of his desire to build more expensive cars.

Malcomson was outraged, threatened to sue, and then made a fatal mistake. He announced he was also going to form a new company, one that would build cars. But the directors pointed out that he couldn't be involved in two competing companies at once. The newly formed Ford Manufacturing Company was committed to being a supplier to the original Ford Motor Company, but Malcomson was involved in a clear conflict of interest. On December 6, 1905, the day after the newspapers announced that Malcomson's new company was created, Ford Motor Company asked Malcomson to resign. He refused, but he eventually saw the handwriting on the wall. The profits on the new Model N could easily flow to the Ford Manufacturing Company as the maker of its key parts. The Ford Motor Company would cease to be such a profitable investment. By May of 1906, Malcomson had sold his stock back to the company. His few supporters left over the next year.

The new Ford Manufacturing Company was folded into the Ford Motor Company. Henry Ford was now the majority stockholder and was essentially free to do what he wanted, which was to focus on the Model N and ultimately build a cheap car to be sold in unprecedented quantities. The way was now clear for the coming of the Model T in 1908, a car that would revolutionize the automobile business.

June 29, 1906— The Interstate Commerce Commission (ICC) got a big boost when the Hepburn Act was passed. The act, authored by Senator W.P. Hepburn, permitted the ICC to set "just and reasonable" maximum rates for the railroads. Thus, after 20 years of existence, the ICC was given the crucial power it needed to rein in the railroads. This marked a true turning point in the ICC's ability to control the railroads, giving the commission a power it would use to dramatic effect for much of the rest of the century.

Ironically, so strong was anti-railroad sentiment in the country, especially in the middle west, that Senator Hepburn, who was born in Ohio and grew up in Iowa, lost his next election for not doing more to control the railroads.

March 19, 1908— The first circulars describing the new Ford car, the Model T, were sent out to Ford dealers. One purpose of the circular was to give dealers time to clear their stocks of older models before the Model T deliveries began in October of 1908. The Model N had been highly popular since it was introduced in 1906, and a Model R and Model S were added to the line as slightly upscale versions of the Model N, while the older expensive Model K was being phased out.

As sales of the Model N increased, the company was learning to build high volumes of new cars as efficiently as possible. On June 4, 1908, Ford workers set a record by building 101 automobiles in one ten-hour day (the standard workday at that time) in the process of filling the last of the Model N and Model S orders in preparation to begin work on the Model T at the end of the summer. The advent of the Model T meant not only the development of a car that had superior engineering and materials, it meant the development of practices and processes that enabled low costs to be achieved in volume production, and thus low prices to be achieved in the marketplace.

The development of the Model T began in the winter of 1906-07, when Henry Ford had a room built on the top floor of the factory, away from manufacturing activities. The room was about 12 feet by 15 feet, and it soon became home for Ford and several key designers and draftsmen. He moved a rocking chair that used to belong to his mother into the room, and used to sit there for long hours while he discussed and thought about problems.

In 1907, Henry Ford made a declaration describing his vision of what his new car would be:

> I will build a motor car for the great multitude. It will be large enough for the whole family, but small enough for the individual to run and care for. It will be constructed of the best materials, by the best men to be hired, after the simplest designs that modern engineering can devise. But it will be so low in price that no man making a good salary will be unable to own one — and enjoy with his family the blessings of hours of pleasure in God's great open spaces.

By the end of a year, as 1907 was giving way to 1908, the men in the room were working late every day. When the new experimental car emerged from the little room and was taken on a test drive, Henry Ford was exultant. The car now met all of his goals for a low-cost but solid car that could be cheaply manufactured in quantity.

The body of the Model T was lifted high off the ground so it could be driven in fields and other rough terrain. It had a four-cylinder vertical engine that generated 20 horsepower, and Ford had replaced the batteries found in other cars with a magneto to fire the spark plugs. It was built using vanadium steel, which was very strong but also known for its relatively light weight. The wheelbase was only eight feet, four inches, making the car very compact, and it weighed only 1200 pounds.

The basic price was $825, not yet spectacularly low (it would eventually fall to less than half that price), but as Ford advertisements correctly said, "no car under $2,000 offers more, and no car over $2,000 offers more except in trimming." The car was an immediate success, especially with farmers. Orders poured in even before the official October 1, 1908, availability date, and by May 1, 1909, the company announced it had enough orders to consume the factory output through August, and they had to stop accepting new orders temporarily. Henry Ford had built just the right car for the times. Now he needed a way to greatly increase production of the car. Ford turned his attention to that problem next.

August 8, 1908 — This Saturday in August, Wilbur Wright was preparing to demonstrate the latest version of the Wright brothers' Flyer before a crowd of a few hundred gathered at the racetrack near Le Mans, France. This was the culmination of over four years of effort since the brothers had achieved the first manned flight at Kitty Hawk on December 17, 1903. The patent pursued by the brothers had finally been awarded in 1906, and they felt they were still several years ahead of the competition. They had made a number of successful flights around Dayton in the past few years, and they took a hard line in trying to cash in on their invention. They refused reasonable offers asking for a demonstration before they got a contract, insisting instead on a contract first, which would be made subject to a successful demonstration. This chicken-and-egg contractual problem, and the fact that they tried to sell their very expensive (for the time) $25,000 machine by writing letters rather than marketing it in person, had delayed success until the year of 1908, when they had not one, but two contracts.

One contract was from the United States Signal Corps, for which they would make demonstrations in September of 1908. The other contract was with a French concern interested in building planes under license, and this was the contract for which Wilbur was preparing to fly on this August afternoon. The brothers realized that the timing of the contracts was such that one would have to fly in France while the other would have to stay behind and perform the demonstrations for the Signal Corps in the United States. The brothers were normally inseparable, but this was the long-awaited chance of a lifetime, so they built two Flyers and set out to demonstrate both of them.

Wilbur had been waiting for good weather since the previous Wednesday, when he had finally finished assembling the Flyer, a job that had taken almost seven weeks rather than the three weeks he had estimated. But this Saturday was finally the day. Many in the crowd were still wondering if the Wright brothers were really some sort of gigantic fraud. The brothers had worked in such secrecy while they were trying to obtain their patent and a contract to sell their Flyer that relatively few people had actually seen them in the air. Finally, at 6:30 in the afternoon, the engine was started, and moments later the Flyer virtually leaped into the air after its brief run down the launching rail.

The crowd was immediately astounded. In France planes commonly hopped and skipped along the ground before getting airborne, and then they made banks and turns with great care, if they banked at all. Wilbur quickly rose into the air, turned sharply to avoid some trees at the end of the racecourse, and then easily completed two full circuits within the cramped confines of the racecourse, bringing the Flyer down on its skids to within 50 feet of where he had started. He was in the air for exactly one minute and forty-five seconds, but that mattered very little to the crowd. The ease and skill with which he flew the Flyer in his customary gray business suit and high starched collar was obvious to everyone in the crowd. They realized that something new had occurred in the field of aviation.

The crowd surged onto the field and surrounded Wilbur and the Flyer. Some pilots who were there gave admiring quotes to listening reporters. Said Paul Zens, who had waited since morning to see the late afternoon flight: "I would have waited ten times as long to have seen what I have seen today.

Mr. Wright has us all in his hands." Rene Gasnier said: "The whole conception of the machine — its execution and its practical worth — is wonderful. We are as children compared to the Wrights." Probably the third most experienced pilot in France, Louis Bleriot, who in 1909 would become the first person to cross the English Channel in an airplane, stated: "I consider that for us in France, and everywhere, a new era in mechanical flight has commenced. I am not sufficiently calm after the event to thoroughly express my opinion."

There were no flights on Sunday, as neither of the Wright brothers had ever flown on the Sabbath. But the French newspaper, *Le Figaro*, was filled with praise for Wilbur and the Wright brothers. For the first time the expression "birdman" was born. Wilbur's flight was called "a revolution in the scientific world." On Monday a crowd of over 2,000 people overflowed the grandstand, in contrast to the few hundred that had been there Saturday.

Wilbur did not disappoint them, even though he made only two flights. The first flight lasted only 42 seconds because Wilbur misjudged the room available to make a full circle, and he found himself heading for some trees at the edge of the course at a height too low to clear them. He made a sudden sharp turn and landed. It was in a sense an aborted flight, but the crowd was ecstatic. They found the sharp turn with a radius of less than 100 feet to be an unbelievable maneuver. Wilbur's second flight was much like the one he made Saturday, two full circuits of the field, but he threw in a figure eight and again the crowd went wild.

A leading figure in French aviation, Leon Delagrange, had specifically come down from Paris to see what the fuss was all about. After watching Wilbur's performance, he said, "It is marvelous, I assure you, marvelous," when asked about the ease with which Wilbur flew the figure eight. The next morning, when approached by a reporter from *Le Matin*, Delagrange shrugged and said: "Oh well, we are beaten. We do not even exist." Actually, these flights at Le Mans were meant to give Wilbur experience with the new Flyer so he would have no trouble with the later final flights required under the contract. Those demonstrations required flights of at least 50 kilometers (30 miles), but they would be much easier to make after the French Army relented and permitted the use of their much larger artillery range at Camp d'Auvours, only seven miles east of Le Mans. The Flyer was moved to the new field, and Wilbur continued to amaze the French, continuing to set world records in the Flyer in subsequent months. A new age of aviation had clearly begun.

September 3, 1908— On this Thursday in the late summer of 1908, Orville Wright took off in his Flyer at Fort Myer, Virginia, just outside Washington, D.C., to begin the performance tests for the Signal Corps contract. The crowd, including President Teddy Roosevelt's son, 20-year-old Theodore Roosevelt, Jr., had the same astonished reaction as Wilbur had produced in

France, but the newspaper coverage was much more restrained, because, frankly, most newspapers did not recognize the difference between Orville's flight and the brief flights of other pilots recently made in the United States.

On Wednesday, September 9th, Orville flew for 57 and a half minutes, breaking the world endurance mark of a little under 30 minutes that had just been set by Leon Delagrange in Paris on Sunday, September 6th. Now the newspapers began to pay attention to what was happening at Ft. Myer. Orville proceeded to set a new record for endurance, height, or both every day for the next four days. Wilbur, in the meantime, was setting European records, even if he was not catching up to Orville's world records. The papers around the world were filled with news about the Wright brothers. Then tragedy struck.

On Thursday, September 17, 1908, Orville took off with a passenger. The contract required the aircraft to be able to carry a passenger, and Orville had done so twice before with members of the Signal Corps. The passenger this time was Lieutenant Tom Selfridge, the next member of the Signal Corps in line for a flight. Soon after taking off Orville heard a strange noise, and the Flyer soon became unmanageable. As became known later, one blade of the right propeller had split. The unequal pressure on the two blades caused a vibration that loosened a stay wire, permitting the propeller axle to turn slightly, which brought the undamaged blade in contact with a stay wire leading to the tail. This wire tore loose, wrapped itself around the propeller blade, and broke it off. The Flyer dove into the ground from a height of about 50 feet. Orville suffered a broken leg, some broken ribs, and a scalp wound. He would recover fully, but about a dozen years later it was discovered that he had three hipbone fractures and a dislocated hip. These injuries would cause him occasional severe pain for the rest of his life. Lieutenant Selfridge suffered a fractured skull, and died after an operation that night to try to save his life. He never regained consciousness, and became the first person in history to be killed in an accident involving a propeller-driven flying machine.

The Signal Corps had been very impressed by what they had seen so far, and they extended the date for the fulfillment of the contract demonstrations until the end of June 1909. In the meantime, Wilbur continued winning plaudits in France, and on the last day of the year, Wilbur flew for over two hours and twenty minutes, flying about 150 kilometers (90 miles) in total. About two weeks earlier, he had set a world altitude record of 361 feet. These flights were made to win various prizes, including 20,000 francs for the longest endurance flight by the end of the year, and at the end of 1908, Wilbur had broken every important aircraft record, including several of his own. With the Signal Corps contract Orville would obtain the following June, the Wright brothers would dominate the aviation world for almost a year. Then the decline would begin.

September 16, 1908 — In addition to the introduction of the Model T by Henry Ford and the exploits of the Wright brothers, a third event occurred in 1908 that would have a major impact on transportation in the United States, but it was little noted at the time. On this day, William Crapo (Billy) Durant filed incorporation papers for a holding company to be called General Motors. After Henry Ford, Durant was probably the most notable figure in the automobile business in the first two decades of the 20th century.

Durant, then 46, was born in 1862, one year before Henry Ford. He was born in Boston, but raised in Michigan under the careful eye of his grandfather, ex–Governor H.H. Crapo. Durant died on March 18, 1947, only a few weeks before Henry Ford. They were true contemporaries, and founded the two biggest automobile companies in the world (which they still are today), General Motors and the Ford Motor Company. The history of these two companies is the history of the automobile industry. Yet few people noticed when Durant died, while the death of Henry Ford three weeks later was a national event. Such are the vagaries of fame.

Durant made his fortune selling carriages and wagons. His Durant-Dort company sold 150,000 a year around the turn of the century. In 1904, he took over the struggling Buick Company, refinanced it, and sold 1,400 Buicks in 1906, 4,600 in 1907, and 8,800 in 1908, second only to Henry Ford. Early in 1908, Durant had gotten the four biggest car sellers together (Henry Ford and Durant, Ransom Olds — creator of the early Oldsmobile and now making the Reo, and Benjamin Briscoe, builder of the Maxwell) to discuss forming a giant joint combination that would tower over all other manufacturers. After continuing discussions throughout the year, Henry Ford and his tough business manager, James Couzens, demanded a payment of $3 million in cash as being "more equal" than the others. Ransom Olds then demanded the same, and the talks came to an end.

Durant continued with his idea, but J.P. Morgan, who was to supply financial backing for the new firm, dropped out because he heard Durant talking about the industry ultimately producing half a million cars a year. Morgan decided Durant was too wildly optimistic to be trusted as a competent investor. No one imagined how closely Durant was to the mark. Finally, Durant decided to go it alone. On this date, he started the new holding company, and then looked for car companies to comprise it.

Besides his own Buick Company, he added Cadillac, the original Oldsmobile Company that Ransom Olds had parted with when the owners wanted to build more expensive cars than Olds was interested in, and finally the new Oakland, which eventually became the Pontiac. Other car and parts builders were also brought under the shell of the General Motors Corporation. Durant was a tireless promoter and con man, and he claimed his new company would build a car for every taste and pocketbook, just the opposite of Henry Ford.

Durant's frantic game would soon fall apart as the company was taken over by the bankers, but he would be back again, bigger and brasher than ever.

July 30, 1909— On this Friday, officially the last day of demonstrations required by the Signal Corps contract, Orville Wright was ready to complete the last part of the contract specifications, the speed test. In the preceding days he had completed the other requirements of the contract, breaking Wilbur's record for two-man flight duration in the process. The speed test also required that a passenger be carried, and the speed was determined by flying to a nearby town (more than five miles away for at least a round trip of ten miles) whose distance away on the ground was accurately known. Then the time to complete the trip, with allowances for turns, was carefully measured to calculate the speed. The Wrights would be paid a bonus for speeds above 40 miles per hour, and be charged a penalty for speeds under 40 miles per hour.

Before a crowd of about 7,000 spectators, including President Taft, Orville took off at 6:46 P.M. with Lieutenant Benjamin Foulois (later a major general and chief of the U.S. Army Air Corps), and headed for Alexandria, Virginia, about five miles away. Orville returned at 7:08 and immediately a number of official stopwatches were read to average their readings and calculate the speed. The next day the official speed was announced as 42.58 miles per hour, netting the Wrights a bonus of $5,000, for a total price of $30,000 for the first Flyer purchased by the government. Some more exhibition flights were made in 1909, but by the end of the year the Wright brothers announced they were done with flying in public. Other business efforts awaited their attention.

August 18, 1909— The first patent infringement claim was filed by the Wright brothers against Glenn Curtiss, another true pioneer of the early aviation business. This would begin nearly a decade-long battle between the brothers and Curtiss. The battles over patent infringements would end when government pressure forced an industry-wide settlement after the United States entered World War I, in 1917. Orville Wright was especially bitter about the issue, because he felt Curtiss and his associates had stolen secrets from the Wright brothers during visits to Kitty Hawk before 1903, and in subsequent communications between the two parties. This bitterness made any sort of settlement between the parties impossible until the government took action. Eventually the Curtiss Company became very successful, and the Curtiss-Wright Corporation that was formed in the 1920s was so named because the Curtiss Company was the much larger of the two at the time.

November 22, 1909— The Wright Company was incorporated, with J.P. Morgan acting as one of the prime backers. The Wright brothers received

$100,000 in cash, one-third of the stock, and a 10 percent royalty on each plane sold. The brothers had indeed cashed in in a big way on their invention. But aside from becoming rich, their lives were much less satisfactory from this point onward than they anticipated. In four years Wilbur would be dead of typhoid fever, and Orville, who hated being a businessman instead of an inventor, would sell out his interest in just six years. The Wright brothers would disappear from the scene as aviation became a much bigger part of the world than anyone had ever anticipated when they made their historic flight in 1903.

January 1, 1910— The first formal move into Ford's new Highland Park factory took place on this date. As the old year wound down, all cars were being shipped from the old Piquette Street plant. When the new year opened, a good percentage were being shipped from the new plant in Highland Park. Department by department, the new plant opened during the first part of 1910. The new plant was designed by famed architect Albert Kahn. It was in this plant that Ford and his engineers would develop the moving assembly line that would revolutionize the manufacturing of cars — and many other products.

The huge sales of the Model T made a new plant absolutely necessary for the Ford Motor Company. Sales were 10,607 for the 1908-09 year, 18,664 in 1909-10, and 34,528 for 1910-11. They would climb to 78,440 in 1911-12, then pass 100,000 with a total of 168,304 in 1912-13. Even J.P. Morgan would have to confess that Billy Durant knew what he was talking about when forecasting eventual total industry sales of a half million per year (*see entry for* September 16, 1908) when Ford alone hit 248,307 in 1913-14. Durant's Buick remained close to Ford for a few years, but when Ford soared to almost the 250,000 mark in 1913-14, the nearest competitor was Willys-Overland, with less than one-fifth of the Ford total. Eventually, in the 1923 sales year, Ford would sell over 2 million cars, accounting for 57 percent of the cars sold in the United States, and about half of the cars sold in the world. For the 15 years after the Model T was introduced, it really was the automotive market all by itself. No car has since approached the market domination the Model T achieved in 1923. It had practically no competition until Chevrolet began to nip at its heels after 1925.

The moving assembly line developed at Highland Park permitted much higher assembly rates and lower prices per car, which meant even more sales and Ford climbed high above the competition. Henry Ford said that the secret of the assembly line was its constant sub-division of labor into smaller and smaller pieces: "The man who places a part does not fasten it. The man who puts in a bolt does not put on the nut; the man who puts on the nut does not tighten it." The number of man-hours to complete a chassis fell from twelve and a half hours to 93 minutes. The price of the basic Model T fell from $850 at its introduction in 1908 to $440 in 1914 and then to $390 and $345 in the following two years. No one could compete with these prices, and the Model T continued to outsell every car in the world. Henry Ford had done just what he said he would do.

September 25, 1910— This was the first day of a series of meetings that ended with Billy Durant losing control of General Motors Corporation to his bankers. The bankers helped to pull the corporation together by instituting disciplined control of management and finances. They originally planned to liquidate the company or possibly reduce it to its Buick roots, but a favorable report from the Cadillac branch convinced them to save the whole company. However, the price was high, in the form of a loan with very stringent terms and the removal of any real power from Durant. The conservatism of the bankers led to eventual stockholder unrest because of the low dividends paid on the common stock. The settlement was good for the bankers and the preferred stockholders, but not for the holders of the common stock. That left an opening for Durant to return.

In the fall of 1910, Durant got together with the Swiss-born star of Buick's racing team, Louis Chevrolet, to build a new car that he would use as the basis to retake General Motors in five years. He was always confident that with his ability to raise money, plus his own personal fortune, he would eventually succeed. Thus, in the fall of 1910, the last big piece of General Motors was put into place, even if it was done outside the company per se, when Durant took the first step in building the Chevrolet Motor Company.

January 9, 1911— Henry Ford won an important court case that affected both the future of the Ford Motor Company and the entire automotive industry. Ford was successful in appealing a court decision made in 1909 granting George Selden patent rights, essentially, on anything called a horseless carriage. The decision made on this date found that the 1909 decision was invalid, and Selden's patent claims were thrown out in a way that assured there would be no further appeals.

George Selden was a lawyer with some inventor-like characteristics who had filed a patent for a "motor carriage" in 1879. But he had deliberately delayed issuance of the patent, as was permitted then, by constantly adding "improvements." It appears that Selden did not really intend to build what he later called a horseless carriage, but simply to delay the beginning of the patent until he had a better idea of what such a device would look like so that he could claim to have patented it. He was officially granted a patent in 1895, more than 16 years after his initial filing.

Selden signed an agreement to sell the patent for $10,000, plus a royalty on all patent claims the company buying the patent could collect. The first few carmakers approached decided to pay royalties while forming the Association of Licensed Automobile Manufacturers, or the ALAM. In essence, they would approve other manufacturers who wished to join, thus cutting themselves in on the riches Selden hoped to win while controlling to some extent their competition.

When the Ford Motor Company was founded in 1903, some initial meetings ended with one in which James Couzens, Ford's hard-nosed business manager, told the ALAM what Selden could do with his patent. When told this was a foolish answer and that the Selden group could put Ford out of business, Henry Ford challenged them to try. On October 22, 1903, a patent infringement suit was filed against Ford.

For the next six years, the legal battle took its usual tortuous course. Ford's position was basically that the patent did not describe a buildable car, and, in fact, Selden had never built one. On December 15, 1909, a verdict was rendered in favor of Selden, but Ford immediately appealed. New arguments began on November 22, 1910, just as Model T production was approaching new highs in the Highland Park plant.

On January 9, 1911, a new verdict was read in favor of Henry Ford. Selden has basically guessed wrong about how the final gasoline engines used in cars built in the 1900s would operate. His patent was valid only for cars using the old Brayton engine, which no car manufacturer ever did. Ford was completely victorious.

After the decision, Ford became looked upon for the first time as a folk hero. He had taken on all of the other major car manufacturers and won. In the meantime he was churning out the Model T, a car for the common man, not a toy for the rich. It was one of the first steps towards Henry Ford becoming a legend.

February 11, 1911 — The first electric self-starter passed all of its acceptance tests at the Cadillac Motor Car company. It appeared in the 1912 Cadillac (and in the cars of many other manufacturers soon after), and its official appearance in the marketplace signaled the end of the electric car and the steamer as alternative modes of automobile design. Primarily, the self-starter made the gasoline engine usable by anyone — female or male, young or old, strong or weak. That eliminated the major advantage of the electric car. This enabled the gasoline engine to become so firmly entrenched that when Abner Doble designed a great new version of the steamer in the late teens and early 1920s, it was too late to penetrate the car market in any significant way.

The self-starter was designed by Charles F. Kettering, who was a 32-year-old engineer with National Cash Register in 1908 (that magic year again) when a friend told him about problems Cadillac (and other car companies) were having with electric ignition systems used to fire spark plugs. Kettering went to work on the problem in his spare time, sold 8,000 ignition sets to Cadillac, and turned the barn he had been working in into the Dayton Engineering Laboratories Company (the Wright brothers were not the only engineering geniuses in Dayton at the time), a company which soon became known as Delco. Kettering went on to develop a number of other electric system improvements for automobiles, and he became the key research guru in the business when his company was later acquired by General Motors.

July 1, 1911— The first airplane sale to the Navy was made, by Glenn Curtiss. Interested in seaplanes for many years, Curtiss was later dubbed the "Father of Naval Aviation." His so-called hydroaeroplane was outside the strictures of the patent battle he was having with the Wright brothers. His plane could take off or land on water, and was demonstrated February 17, 1911, at San Diego. The cruiser Pennsylvania hoisted the plane on board from the water on which it had landed, so it could repeat its ability to take off and land on water when it was once again lowered into the ocean. It was the birth of the seaplane.

Five months later, after improvements had been made to the basic design, the Navy purchased a model that could take off and land on either land or water, using retractable wheels. It was called the Triad, and designated the A-1 by the Navy. Now both the Army and Navy had airplanes of their own, one from the Wright brothers and one from Curtiss, the key American pioneers of flight.

May 29, 1912— Wilbur Wright died of typhoid fever at the age of 45. It essentially meant the end of the involvement of the Wright brothers in the field of aviation. Wilbur had been President of the Wright Company, and now the mantle fell on the shoulders of Orville, who preferred inventing to dealing with business details. He especially hated dealing with the problems concerning the patent war going on with Glenn Curtiss, whom he hated with a passion. The Wright brothers had won an initial court decision on January 3, 1910, and would win again on January 13, 1914. But the same lawyer who won the Selden case (*see entry for* January 9, 1911) was then hired by Curtiss to try again.

Henry Ford put in his oar for Curtiss because he thought the patent suits by the Wright brothers were meant to hold down competition in the aviation field, just as the Selden patent attempted to do among automobile companies. As noted before, the patent issue would disappear with the entry of the United States into World War I in 1917, but for now it was producing great pain for Orville, who felt the issue and its stress had contributed to Wilbur's death. In 1913, Orville began making plans to get out of the business entirely. In the spring of 1914, he quietly began to buy up stock to gain control of the company.

July 1, 1913— The Lincoln Highway Association was formed. Their announced purpose was to "produce the establishment of a continuous improved highway from the Atlantic to the Pacific [New York to San Francisco], open to lawful traffic of all descriptions without toll charges." The idea became very popular, but acting upon the idea proved very difficult, as it would for many future highway schemes.

There was pressure from various localities to run the road through their community rather than the planned ones; problems with financing (the estimated costs were $10 million dollars) to the extent that it was decided instead to install a policy of cooperation with communities willing to build pieces of the road; problems with the maintenance of building standards; disagreements between states and their communities; and even arguments about the proper marking of the road. It was frustrating, but actually good experience and education for road-building tasks to come.

The road was never completed under its original name, although many sections of it were built under different highway route numbers. But the concept was firmly established. In 1915 Congress appropriated $75 million for matching funds for states who would contribute to highway building projects. The amounts would grow, and people would soon come to realize that an extensive highway system, comparable to the railroad system, was something the nation needed. The roadbuilding phase in America's history really began on this July day, even if there was a long way yet to go.

January 5, 1914— The Ford Motor Company announced what was to become known as the "five-dollar day." In one stroke, Ford would practically double the average pay, and at the same time reduce his workers' nine-hour day to eight hours. The Highland Park plant could now go to three eight-hour shifts, working around the clock to meet the seemingly insatiable demand for the Model T. The reality of the situation was much more complex than the newspaper headlines after the announcement made it appear.

Worker turnover had become a big problem at Ford. By one estimate it had reached 380 percent through December of 1913, meaning that 963 men had to be hired to keep 100. The company directors had decided to issue a Christmas bonus for men who had been with the company for three years, and found that only about four percent of the workforce qualified. Assembly line work was monotonous, and at Ford pressure was applied to keep the pace up and costs down. It was hoped the five-dollar day would help solve this problem. The extra payment in wages was considered a "profit sharing" bonus, which would be bigger than the basic wage, but the worker had to put in at least six months work to earn the bonus. Further, the worker had to be over 22 years old unless married or supporting a widowed mother or next-of-kin. Other requirements buried in the small print would hopefully improve the quality of the average worker hired.

A "Sociological Department" was created at Ford, to ensure that workers were living in a way that Henry Ford approved of and thus were deserving of the bonus. The department made visits to the workers' homes and got otherwise involved in their personal lives to be sure they were living in an "appropriate" way. Henry Ford insisted that the increased wage was one of the greatest cost-saving moves he had ever made. English-language courses were started after working hours to help those workers (71 percent of the Ford workforce was not born in America) who needed help to speak English. The experiment in paternalism rose to new heights as Ford emphasized the need to live in the way he approved, using the bonus as the carrot. At any rate, for some years he got — or thought he got — the improved workforce he was looking for. It wasn't lost on Ford that he was creating more potential buyers of the Model T by increasing the wages of his workers. In a later court case challenging his practice of continually reducing the price of his cars rather than paying out more dividends, he stated:

> Every time you reduce the price of the car without reducing the quality, you increase the possible number of purchasers. There are many men who will pay $360 for a car who would not pay $440. We had in round numbers 500,000 buyers of cars on the $440 basis, and I figure that on the $360 basis we could increase the sales to possibly 800,000 cars for the year — less profit on each car, but more cars, more employment of labor, and in the end we get all the profit we ought to make.

But all of this was in the future on the day the announcement of the five-dollar day was made. The newspapers got the news in the afternoon of January 5, 1914. By two o'clock the next morning, men began gathering around the employment office at the Highland Park plant. By dawn, masses of men had filled the streets, and about ten thousand men left in an angry mood when a "No Hiring" sign was posted. The next day public notices were posted that no hiring was yet taking place, but another huge crowd gathered, many from other cities nearby. The company announced that men who formed crowds would not be considered, so on the third day the crowds milled loosely on the streets near the factory. Ford agents surreptitiously circulated among the men handing out slips to some for admission to the employment office. But word circulated that hiring was actually beginning, and on Friday 15,000 men appeared in the streets near the plant.

The city began to get deeply concerned about the crowds surrounding the Ford plant. Reporters came out in droves, drawn by the report the numerous poignant stories of people who had risked everything to seek employment at Ford. But they also published stories warning people from other cities not to come to Detroit. On Saturday large signs in several languages appeared at the plant saying all hiring had ceased, and the crowd was down to a manageable four thousand.

By 7:30 Monday morning, however, 10,000 men had again massed in front of the factory. This time a riot ensued as Ford workers wearing Ford badges tried to push through the crowd to get to work. The crowd surged against the gates and the police, and hundreds broke free and ran into the plant. Finally, a fire hose was turned on the mob, and in weather only nine degrees above zero, the mob dissolved, smashing a number of lunch stands in the area as they left. Better planning might have helped, but no one anticipated the number of workers in the Detroit area who would be desperate for new jobs, even though the pay rate was the highest in American history for the type of job being offered.

The Ford Company announced that it had already received 14,000 letters of application. It would stop all hiring for the moment, and in any event it would not hire anyone who had not lived in Detroit for six months. Recruitment would be turned over to the Employers' Association. The crowds abated, and the workers inside the plant were elated at their good luck. Most received credit for the time they had already worked at Ford, and were soon earning the new pay rate. Other automobile companies eventually moved to match the Ford Motor Company, so Henry Ford's action essentially created a new minimum wage for the entire industry. Henry Ford had taken another step towards becoming a folk hero.

In his field Ford was undoubtedly a genius, and his vision of the future was one of the Ford Motor Company's greatest assets. But he was otherwise an uneducated man, and when he stepped into fields where he had no background or training, such as politics and race relations, he did a great deal of damage. Ultimately, his autocratic form of management, and his refusal to listen to other views, almost drove his company into bankruptcy in the 1940s, and led to the tragic early death, at age 50, of his only son in 1943. But in 1914, and for the next decade, he was king of his world.

September 16, 1915 — A board meeting of General Motors took place, at which it was planned to renew the trust agreement of 1910 and appoint a new board of directors. Billy Durant was asked before the meeting started not to cause any trouble, and he had what must have been the huge satisfaction of replying that there would not be any renewal of the trust agreement, but there wouldn't be any trouble because he now had enough stock to control General Motors.

Durant had been quietly buying shares of stock in the open market with his own personal fortune. The price was reasonable because the bankers refused to pay any dividends on the common stock, plowing profits back into the company and paying dividends only to the preferred stockholders. In the meantime, sales of Durant's Chevrolet were booming, and when he created the Model 490, which all car buyers realized was named after the selling price of the Model T, the price of the Model T was lowered to $440. Durant was at least trying to compete with Ford in lower-price cars, a field which General Motors had been criticized for ignoring. When Durant offered 500 shares of Chevrolet stock for 100 shares of General Motors stock, he was oversubscribed to the point that his office in New York had to store the General Motors shares in bushel baskets.

At the meeting, Durant blocked the renewal of the bankers' control, and got the board to declare a dividend, the first since the bankers had taken control in 1910. New directors were nominated, including Pierre S. du Pont and his lieutenant John J. Raskob, who would have much to do with the future of General Motors. It would take until 1916 to finalize the details, but the minnow (Chevrolet, with sales of less the $10 million) swallowed the whale (General Motors, with sales of more than $94 million).

Notably, during Durant's tenures, Charles W. Nash, who later started the Nash automobile company, and Walter P. Chrysler, who started the Chrysler automobile corporation, were alternately in charge of Buick and General Motors. Alfred P. Sloan, Jr., came to General Motors in 1916 and ultimately stayed on to become its president when Durant left for the last time in 1920. Thus, all the major players in the automobile industry (including Henry Ford) that was created in the first decades of the century had been involved in Billy Durant's successes and failures between 1908 and 1920. After Henry Ford, in his way Billy Durant was the most influential leader in launching the automobile industry, and in turning it into the nation's largest by the 1920s.

October 15, 1915 — The Wright Company was sold to a group of eastern capitalists headed by William B. Thompson, a mining tycoon. Orville became a consultant to the new company at a salary of $25,000 per year. He had a small laboratory in Dayton, only half a block from the old bicycle shop. Ten months after Orville sold out, his company was merged with the Martin Company, and the Wright-Martin Aircraft Corporation got a World War I contract for airplane motors (the war had started in Europe in 1914), and the company moved its manufacturing operations to New Jersey. Thus, the Wright brothers left their home base of Dayton, and left aviation in general (except for a Wright-Dayton company founded during the war that actually had very little to do with the Wrights, other than Orville's willingness to let his name be used). In retrospect, the brothers had been at the top for only a brief time, but it was a brilliant show while it lasted.

The Curtiss Aeroplane and Motor Corporation became the biggest aircraft manufacturer in the United States, and now held patents of its own that required they take legal action to collect license fees from other companies. When the United States entered World War I in April of 1917, the government forced a cross-licensing agreement on all the aircraft companies, ending the patent battles for good, with a payment of $2 million each to Wright-Martin and Curtiss for their trouble.

March 5, 1917— Inauguration Day in 1917, upon which President Wilson started his second term in office. He was the last president to ride in a carriage to his inauguration; future presidents would make the trip in an automobile. In 1916, the nation's railroads had reached an historical peak of 254,036 miles of track. This was 31 percent more than in 1900, but from 1917 onward the total would fall, shrinking by almost 50 percent to under 132,000 miles by 2000. In 1916, railroads carried 98 percent of all passenger traffic service, but, they had fallen on hard economic times. Government regulation and taxes were finally having an effect.

President Wilson was furious with the railroads on Inauguration Day. He had forced a settlement to avoid a union strike over the demand for an eight-hour day. The Adamson Act, requested by Wilson, legislated the eight-hour day as of January, 1917, but the railroads sued in the Supreme Court. The Adamson Act was upheld on March 21, 1917, just a little over two weeks after Wilson was inaugurated. Essentially, this act gave Congress unquestioned authority over the railroads.

Wilson's anger at the railroads was over more than this one issue. He knew when he was inaugurated that within a month the country would enter World War I, and the need to transport troops and materials to East Coast ports would become critical. The railroads were operating in some disarray at the time, yet even in hard times they continued to act as if cooperating with the government was beneath them. By the end of the year Wilson had to seize control of the railroads to stop the endless bickering among the owners, both among themselves and with the government.

By contrast, the automotive industry was doing all it could to cooperate in the crisis. To ease the burden on the overloaded railroads, the industry agreed to drive over 30,000 trucks, intended for service in Europe, directly from Midwestern plants to the East Coast. The winter turned out to be especially severe, and crews went out to clear snow drifts as the trucks bumped along clearly inadequate roads. As America prepared to enter World War I, the story was the same. The railroads were grumpy and uncooperative, and the automotive industry did everything it could to help.

If there was a single point at which Washington began to reach out and help the automotive industry, while contemptibly allowing the railroad business to languish in comparison, it was the Inauguration of Woodrow Wilson for his second term in 1917. From that time on, for the next several decades, money poured out of Washington to build new roads (Wilson had already signed the Federal Road Act of 1916, on July 11, 1916), while the railroads received only more burdensome regulations and taxes. It was not just the comeuppance for the railroads for their decades of arrogance, but a recognition that the country needed more flexible and faster response to transportation crises than the railroads could provide. For most of the rest of the century, automotive transportation would be favored over railroad transportation, until the nation began to strangle on a glut of cars, and by then it was too late to reverse the trend.

May, 1920— During this month the first blast furnace was fired up at the site of Henry Ford's gigantic Rouge River manufacturing plant. Only the blast furnaces were ready at this time, but they were a key symbol of Ford's plans. Henry Ford intended to build a factory that would take in iron ore at one end and produce a car from the other. Ford would even have its own steel manufacturing capability. When completed, the plant took over the manufacture of the Model T, and the famous Highland Park plant was closed.

December 1, 1920— Billy Durant's forced resignation from General Motors took effect. It was his last chance at running the company, although he would make some noise in the 1920s with his own car, the "Durant." He had some ups and downs in the stock market during the decade, but the end of the '20s was the beginning of his slide into obscurity.

Durant had been trying to make money in the stock market using the shares of General Motors (GM) as collateral, but an economic downturn in 1920-21 caught him (and many car makers, including Henry Ford) by surprise. Faced with the fact that brokers might force Durant to dump his GM shares and thus drive the market price down catastrophically, the Du Pont family (who owned about one-quarter of GM) and others bailed him out of his loans, but he was forced to resign from the company.

Alfred Sloan became president, and created the modern corporation in terms of management structure. But he kept Durant's concept of a "car for every purpose and purse," as opposed to Henry Ford's approach, one car at a low price for everyone. Ford had been leading in the marketplace since 1908, but by 1926 the Chevrolet was beginning to nip at Ford's heels. Sloan had stopped Chevrolet from being scrapped, as had been recommended by a consultant after the 1921 downturn, because he wanted to maintain a strong presence in the cheap car market. With the help of William S. Knudsen, an embittered ex–Ford employee, Sloan's Chevrolet became the industry leader by 1927. In addition, people now copied GM's management techniques, just as they once copied Ford's design and assembly-line manufacturing techniques. Henry Ford had become an autocratic manager whose decisions no one dared question. As a result Ford almost slid into bankruptcy in the 1940s, while GM became the number one car company in the world by the end of the 1920s, and remained so into the 21st century.

January 4, 1922 — The assets of the Lincoln Automobile Company were sold to Henry Ford. The Lincoln Company had been started by Henry Leland and his son after the senior Leland quit GM and his own Cadillac Automobile Company. Leland left because of a dispute with Billy Durant over doing work for the government during World War I. Durant claimed the war was none of his business and he wanted no part of it. This was another of Durant's mistakes on the road to losing GM for the second and last time in 1920. Leland was a passionate patriot, and Durant had promised Leland that he wouldn't interfere with him when GM was first formed in 1910, with Leland's Cadillac as a prime piece. The success of Cadillac had also played a key role in the banker's decision to keep GM alive in 1912, but in spite of all this, Durant broke his promise. Leland quit in disgust and founded the Lincoln car company, named in honor of Abraham Lincoln, who Leland considered America's most outstanding historical citizen.

With the acquisition by Henry Ford, Leland had traveled almost full circle, having picked up the pieces of Ford's second failure in 1902 and turned it into the Cadillac car company. Leland was a very respected figure in the automotive industry, and when his new Lincoln car company failed in the fall of November, 1921, due to the economic downturn that also finished Durant at GM, many people were unusually concerned over his failure, including his friends, who had put money into the new company.

Henry Ford was seen as a white knight riding to the rescue Leland, but in reality, with his investment, he had taken over a company at a fraction of the cost of starting one. Six months later the Lelands resigned over "interference" from Ford management personnel, and they were out of work again, but they received hundreds of thousands of dollars from the sale, and the Lincoln Car Company stayed in business. It was still in business eighty years later, having produced some of the finest luxury cars ever made in the form of the Lincoln Continental Mark IV and others. The Lincoln company was Henry Ford's only entry into the high-priced market.

October, 1922 — A black-tie dinner for 200 people was held in the grand ballroom of Washington's famous Willard Hotel, across from the White House. The dinner was arranged by the Highway Education Board (HEB), which had its offices next to the Bureau of Public Roads (BPR) in the Willard building. The purpose of the dinner was to provide propaganda (at the time, the word had not gained a negative connotation) about the need for better roads.

Thomas H. "Chief" MacDonald had come to Washington in 1919 from a similar position in Iowa to become chief of the nation's highways. He would stay there for the next 34 years (he was 38 in 1919). More than any-one else, MacDonald was responsible for the success of the federal-state part-nership that built the nation's highways until the Interstate Highway Program started in the 1950s. Built roughly like a fireplug, MacDonald was the kind of person who his family — including his wife — called "Mr." or "Chief." If any adult ever called him "Tom," there's no record of the event.

As Chief of the Bureau of Public Roads, MacDonald worked tirelessly to build a "we" relationship between the federal and state governments. Mac-Donald also worked closely with the automobile, cement, and steel industries, which had a vested interest in building roads. Politics were critical in road building, and he wanted to be sure they would support his positions. Mac-Donald even held the railroads at bay by saying that truckers could never compete with them in long-haul transportation, a statement that was losing validity even before the increase in improved roads in the 1920s.

Also in attendance at the dinner were H.H. Rice, President of the Cadil-lac division of GM; John J. Taggert, U.S. commissioner of education; rep-resentatives of the Granite Block Manufacturer's Association, the National Paving Brick Manufacturer's Association, and the Portland Cement Associ-ation. M.M. McClure of *McClure's Magazine* gave a speech in which he stated that "You can judge a civilization by the condition of its roads…. We know that the English-speaking people made the fundamental inventions that annihilated space."

From this day forward MacDonald was the key figure from whom Con-gress sought advice on road appropriations, and the prime leader of all the factions interested in building roads, including the bureaus of roads of indi-vidual states. Children and their teachers (and the parents of the children) received voluminous materials, awards, and prizes having to do with good roads, and Harvey Firestone and his renowned tire company funded college scholarships for high school students. The children were thoroughly indoc-trinated in the philosophy that good roads were good for the nation (many studied courses, like civil engineering, that would lead to road-building careers), and hopefully the parents would respond positively at the ballot box, approv-ing the requested funding.

The Bureau of Roads were one of the most successful organizations in recent history as far as bringing its message to children. Every possible oppor-tunity was seized to spread the gospel of good roads. MacDonald was a model of probity and was scrupulously honest. His only goal was to build good roads in the nation, and he would do almost anything to accomplish it. He liked to say there were only three major road-building programs in history: the Romans, the French under Napoleon, and the United States under Mac-Donald. As the Highway Act of 1916 was replaced by the Highway Act of 1921, MacDonald took control of the money spigot in Washington. During the next three decades, money would flow from Congress. MacDonald and his many allies would assume the task of getting the roads built. As the road mileage grew, the mileage of railroad tracks shrank because losses forced them to abandon tracks. The government would fully address road construction after World War II, but in the meantime, MacDonald ruled supreme.

July 1, 1924 — The U.S. Mail began flying at night, ushering in the modern concept of airmail. For years, the post office and its contracts were the financial basis of the commercial aircraft industry, but in 1934 all airmail contracts were cancelled due to a high loss of pilots and aircraft. The Air Mail Act of 1934 was then passed, setting the pattern for commercial aviation for years to come. The Interstate Commerce Commission (ICC) got involved, together with the Bureau of Air Commerce, which was responsible for licensing planes and pilots, and for overall air safety.

The result was a reduction in revenue from airmail contracts, but the contracts were no longer crucial, having served their purpose by then, as the airlines soon began to carry passengers under the new regulations and began competing with the railroads and highways for long distance travelers. Mail contracts served as the main source of revenue for fledgling airlines after 1918 (the first mail contract flight was on May 15, 1918) and into the 1920s, while the development of aircraft service as a true transportation option did not occur until the mid–1930s.

May 21, 1927 — Charles Lindbergh, a former airmail pilot, landed in Paris, completing his historic solo flight begun from New York the day before. Lindbergh had made a calculated decision to try to win the $25,000 prize offered by hotelier Raymond Orteig in 1919 for the first nonstop flight from New York to Paris. He organized financial support among friends in St. Louis, ordered a plane named the *Spirit of St. Louis* from T. Claude Ryan in San Diego (the plane was built in only two months), and flew it to New York on a nonstop transcontinental flight, arriving on May 12, 1927. Eight days later he left for Paris.

Lindbergh was widely hailed as a hero in Europe and the United States, and his feat boosted awareness of the possibilities of commercial air travel. Lindbergh soon became a technical advisor to several fledgling airline companies, and he flew exploratory flights to search out possible air routes with his wife, Anne Morrow Lindbergh, who he married in 1929, acting as his copilot and navigator. His work led to the enlargement of the routes flown by American Airlines, Transcontinental Air Transport (forerunner of TWA), and Pan American Airways. Lindbergh was instrumental in the rise of commercial air travel in the 1930s, but he would have later personal difficulties due to the kidnap-murder of his son and his embracement of Germany's air power prior to World War II.

May 27, 1927 — The Ford assembly line produced its fifteen millionth Model T, which was driven the final stretch by Henry and Edsel Ford. There had been rumors for months that Ford was going to come out with a new car, and the day before, on May 26, it had been officially announced. It was announced on the 27th that the Model T assembly line would soon be shut down to begin retooling for the new car. The Model T had officially become a thing of the past. This triggered a spate of newspaper articles and essays about the old "tin lizzie" that many people had come to regard as part of the family. Roughly half the drivers in the country had driven a Model T as their first car, and no one forgets his or her first car. Only news of this import could push Charles Lindbergh and his nonstop flight to Paris just six days earlier out of the newspaper headlines.

The Model T had become obsolete in the eyes of more and more car buyers. General Motors was promoting the idea of "planned obsolescence," and Billy Durant's idea, a car for "every purpose and purse," now held sway in the marketplace. People wanted cars with new features, and GM gave them a new one every year.

As recently as the 1923 model year, the Model T sold over two million cars, capturing 57 percent of the market in the United States and accounting for about half of worldwide car sales. By 1925, Ford was still selling over two million Model Ts, but now its market share was down to 45 percent, and in 1926 its market share was only 34 percent. The GM Chevrolet had increased sales dramatically and now was pressing Ford. Car buyers preferred the smart new features they got every year from Chevrolet, and they were willing to pay a few hundred dollars more to get them. The marketplace for first-time car buyers was saturated, and industry sales were being driven by replacement-car buyers. GM was better positioned than Ford for such buyers, since Ford offered little besides the Model T. The total sales level of 3.6 million cars reached in 1923 would remain flat until the Depression, and total market growth would not start again until 1949.

Ford managers had been pressing Henry Ford for some time to develop a new model, but Ford, in his autocratic way, refused to listen. When it became clear that the Model T was about to lose the sales lead it had held since its introduction in 1908, Henry Ford donned his engineering hat and began to design of a new car. He was approaching his 64th birthday, but he still had his touch as an engineer.

December 2, 1927 — The new Ford Model A (the company's first car, built in 1903, had also been called the Model A, but it was soon replaced by models bearing the successive letters of the alphabet) was introduced in New York City. It was a national event, and overall car sales had fallen in 1927 as people waited to see what Henry Ford would come up with. With the Model T out of production, Chevrolet finally won the sales leadership position for 1927, but Chevrolet sales did not reach the two million car level, as the Model T had done just a few years earlier. No car would do so for over three decades. The introduction of the Model A was as big a story in the nation as Lindbergh's flight to Paris had been back in May.

In the first week after the introduction of the Model A, an incredible 25 million people were estimated to have seen the car, over 20 percent of the nation's population. The car had all the modern touches the Model T lacked, and the basic Model A was priced at $495 (one "stripped" version could be had for $385). The Model A was roughly $100 cheaper than an equivalently equipped Chevrolet. In fact, since it was a little more substantial and heavier then the Model T, the Model A was actually cheaper on a pound-for-pound basis than its famous predecessor.

New orders flooded in, and the Model A Ford sold about 1.5 million cars in the 1929 model year, taking 34 percent of the market, compared to about 20 percent for Chevrolet. But Chevrolet responded with a new six-cylinder engine and retook the sales lead in 1930. From then on Ford had to be content with second place (or worse) for many decades. Ford's management was no longer competitive with that of GM, and soon its cars were not competitive either.

July 31, 1928 — Walter Chrysler, who had walked away from Billy Durant and General Motors at the beginning of the 1920s, struck a deal to take over what remained of the company originally founded by the Dodge brothers. The brothers had played a key role in the founding of and start-up of the Ford Motor Company, and they had done well when they left Ford to start their own car company. However, both John and Horace Dodge had died in the great flu epidemic of 1920, and the bankers to whom their widows had sold out were now ready to get out of the car business.

After five days of intense negotiation, Chrysler formed the Dodge Division of his new Chrysler Corporation, which had been doing well selling the new Chrysler car since 1925. The car called the Chrysler was an outgrowth of work Walter Chrysler had done with Willys-Overland and the Maxwell car company. The Chrysler car had a very peppy six-cylinder high-compression engine that, although expensive, was a match for anything on the road. However, Walter Chrysler realized that GM, his former company, currently had the best corporate model for success in the car industry. A range of models was needed, and that was why Chrysler went after the Dodge business, adding De Soto and Plymouth in 1929.

Thus, by this day in 1928, the titans of the car business were in place. General Motors, Ford, and the Chrysler Corporation would rule the car business in the United States for most of the rest of the 20th century.

July 1, 1933— The first flight of the DC-1 took place. The aircraft was built by the Douglas Aircraft Company (the "DC" stood for "Douglas Commercial") as a prototype for TWA (then known as Transcontinental and Western Air). The airline used it only for promotional purposes, setting several speed records with the plane on nonstop coast-to-coast flights. The slightly revised DC-2 soon followed, on May 11, 1934, and it became widely used by several airlines as a 14-passenger high-quality airplane.

The pièce de résistance arrived 18 months later in the form on the DC-3. It carried 21 passengers, and first flew on December 17, 1935. American Airlines was first to put the DC-3 into service, beginning scheduled trips on June 7, 1936. The DC-3 was a smashing success; in many ways it was the Model T of the airline industry. By 1939, the extremely dependable DC-3 was flying 90 percent of the airline passengers in the world. The DC-3 effectively launched commercial airplane service worldwide. After its debut, airplane travel became a common alternative to travel by car or train.

The DC-3 had a military equivalent called the C-47, versions of which are still flying today. The British called it the Dakota. Every pilot loved the plane because of its ease of handling and its forgiving nature. Pilots could make serious mistakes and the plane still managed to stay in the air. The DC-3 became very popular in Third World countries as it was phased out for passenger service in the United States in favor of jets (freight carriers in the States continued to use the nearly ageless DC-3 long after it ceased carrying passengers), and old DC-3s can probably still be found in service in some parts of the world.

The DC-3 has often been called the world's most successful airliner, and many have designated it as the most significant commercial airplane ever built. In terms of its impact on the creation of a specific transportation sector, and the fondness with which it is remembered, the comparison of the DC-3 to the Model T is an apt one.

February 23, 1934— A competitor with the DC-3 (and the Boeing 247), the Lockheed 10A Electra, was first flown. It could only carry ten passengers and thus sought a niche market below its bigger competitors, Douglas and Boeing. The fact that the Electra was the preferred plane of Amelia Earhart, one of the most famous pilots ever, largely secured its place in history.

Earhart was already famous for transatlantic flights when she became the first woman to fly solo from Honolulu to the American mainland, in 1935. On June 2, 1937, she set out with a navigator in her Electra 10-E (a more powerful version of the 10-A) to become the first woman to fly around the world. She expected to return a month later on July 4, 1937. However, on July 2, 1937, a transmission from her plane was heard near New Guinea, saying that she and her navigator were lost in the vastness of the Pacific and running out of fuel. She was never heard from again. Many theories were put forward as to what happened, but none were ever proved.

Amelia Earhart actually had little significance in the history of transportation. She was a pioneer female pilot, and her ocean-crossing flights were good publicity for the airline industry, beyond her few pioneering flights but her death was a poignant reminder that the newest mode of transportation was very unforgiving of errors. Many more people have died in traffic accidents than in airplane accidents, but the idea of a few people flying into limbo has never lost its compelling sense of mystery.

June 15, 1938— The two most famous luxury trains of the time, the Broadway Limited and the Twentieth Century Limited, had upgraded streamlined models introduced to the public. The trains were already icons of the Pennsylvania Railroad and the New York Central Railroad respectively. The two railroads had been rivals since the Civil War, and in the 1920s and the 1930s, the rivalry became even more intense. Both trains ran at very high speed from their stations in New York and Chicago. The Twentieth Century was famous for rolling out a red carpet for passengers as they approached the train, and the Broadway announced boarding time in Pennsylvania Station with a bugle call at the door of the popular Savarin Restaurant and again at the train's gate. A chorus of Red Caps then sang a further boarding announcement.

Both redesigned trains had upgraded sleeping compartments, dining cars, lounges, and observation cars. The Twentieth Century locomotive had a more rounded bullet-like nose, and it was the more successful service, sometimes running as many as four or five trains at the same time on the same tracks. They were the peak of luxury train service between the nation's two biggest cities, and movies were made about both trains. The railroads, however, were actually in a precarious position.

The Railway Labor Act of 1926 ended the Sherman Anti-Trust Law's application to railroad strikes and generally gave advantages to the unions in such disputes. The Roosevelt administration passed even more laws favorable to unions, and the railroad unions held an additional ace-in-the-hole in that they could easily declare a particular railroad's locomotives "unsafe" should negotiations not be going their way. Overall, railroad unions fared much better than their counterparts in other industries, and their members' salaries placed them in the top one percent of wageworkers in the nation.

Together with regulation problems from the Interstate Commerce Commission, these high labor costs were strangling the railroads. By 1940 railroad track mileage in the nation was down to 233,670 miles, an eight percent decrease from the peak in 1916. More bankrupt railroads meant more abandoned railroad tracks.

The railroads would have one more moment of glory, during World War II. Travel restrictions on cars resulted in the railroads handling 97 percent of all organized military personnel travel, and 91 percent of all military freight. This meant the railroads carried 83 percent of all traffic, military or civilian, in the nation. It would be their last hurrah, as most were headed for bankruptcy in the decades after World War II.

October 10, 1938— The Works Progress Administration (WPA) gave formal notice of its grant to help build the Pennsylvania Turnpike. Just a little over two weeks later, on October 27, 1938, Walter A. Jones, chairman of the turnpike authority, led the turnpike commissioners to a field about 50 miles from Harrisburg, the state capital. The field was to be the eastern terminal of a turnpike built to carry cars and especially trucks over the Allegheny Mountains on their way from Pittsburgh, in the western end of Pennsylvania, eastward across the state to gain easy access to Philadelphia and its environs. In the field, Jones turned the ceremonial spade of earth for what was called his "dreamway."

The turnpike was to be completed by May of 1940, a seemingly impossible task at the time. Presidential politics was a big factor in the decision to build the turnpike, and to build it quickly. President Roosevelt wanted the turnpike complete before the election of 1940 to help throw Pennsylvania's 38 electoral votes into his camp. Roosevelt himself had proposed a network of national toll roads earlier in the 1930s, but the powerful Thomas MacDonald, head of the Bureau of Public Roads, had quashed the idea on the basis that toll roads could never create enough revenue to pay for themselves as long as good free roads were available. Both men had been impressed by Hitler's autobahns in Germany, but had drawn different conclusions from them. The objectivity of MacDonald's opinion is unclear, as he generally did not favor any road building that might take place outside of his control. He did at least say that toll roads in congested places in the Northeast, like Pennsylvania, might pay for themselves over long periods of time.

That left an opening for Pennsylvania, which wanted a road to cut the terrible travel time over the Alleghenies, especially for trucks (and cars caught behind them). Pennsylvania had another unique advantage that was provided, ironically, by the long competition between the New York Central and Pennsylvania railroads. Back in 1883, when the Pennsylvania Railroad built a line parallel to that of the New York Central up the Hudson River in New York,

Commodore Vanderbilt of the New York Central retaliated by starting construction of a line through the Allegheny Mountains in Pennsylvania, to compete with the Pennsylvania Railroad in its home state. Vanderbilt's new line was almost complete in 1885 when J.P. Morgan, worried about a ruinous rate war that might spread to other railroads, got the two railroads to call off their forays into each other's backyard, and "Vanderbilt's Folly," as it was known locally, was discontinued. It laid unused for 50 years until Pennsylvania state officials began to consider using the abandoned tunnels and right-of-way as a way to save money while building a new turnpike.

The Roosevelt administration immediately recognized that whether MacDonald approved or not, the Pennsylvania Turnpike could qualify as a project under the Works Progress Administration. Jones was very familiar with the ins and outs of Washington, D.C., and to the administration the thought of a big construction project in Pennsylvania that would employ thousands of men at the site and thousands more in the nation's factories was truly irresistible. So with over two-thirds of the funding ultimately available from the Federal Government, construction of the turnpike officially began on this date.

The engineering requirements for the construction of the Pennsylvania Turnpike were at a higher level than had ever been attempted. Grades could not exceed a certain maximum level, and curves had to permit specified high speeds with great safety. As a result the turnpike marched nearly straight across the land, leveling the hills and straightening the curves as much as possible. The engineering specifications and building techniques were the model for the many turnpikes that would follow across the nation. It required working steadily through two winters and two springs in the harsh weather of Pennsylvania, but the turnpike was able to officially open on October 1, 1940, well ahead of the elections.

It was an immediate success. Newspaper reporters, Washington congressmen, the military, and a fleet of cars from General Motors came out to see it and test it in the late summer of 1940. Even Thomas MacDonald, head of the Bureau of Public Roads and an opponent of toll roads, cooperated fully once it was started and called it "a magnificent accomplishment that will be a monument to the foresight of its builders." There were traffic jams of motorists who wanted to try the road out, even though it opened at 12:01 in the morning. During its first year, even with war overseas and rumors of war everywhere, the turnpike was used by an average of 6,500 people a day, nine times what MacDonald had estimated. In September of 1940, before the turnpike was even officially opened, Washington experts, including Thomas MacDonald, said it was "imperative" to extend the turnpike to Philadelphia and the Philadelphia Navy Yard. By the end of the decade, in spite of World War II, turnpikes were springing up in every state in the Northeast. And in every case, they generated revenue in excess of forecasts as soon as they opened. There were also plenty of revenue to adequately maintain the roads. A new era in road building had begun, and would lead to the Interstate Highway System in the 1950s.

January, 1941— The statistics for U.S. urban mass transit patronage through 1940, released this month, showed an important transition in urban transportation over the past several decades. The electrification of streetcar transportation services in American cities, led by Frank J. Sprague, had peaked in the early 1920s. In fact, total transit system ridership of all kinds peaked in 1926 (except for the unique year of 1946, when people were still forced onto public transportation due to the slow lifting of wartime restrictions on automobiles). With the anomalous exception of 1946, 1926 remained the peak year for total transit riders even as the U.S. population doubled by 1990. That is one indication of how thoroughly the automobile took over the transportation sector.

In 1926, mass transit carried totals of 13 billion electric streetcar/trolley riders, 2 billion bus riders, and 2.4 billion rapid transit riders (subways and elevated lines). By 1940, there were less than 6 billion electric streetcar/trolley riders, nearly 5 billion bus riders, and the same 2.4 billion rapid transit riders (mostly in New York, Chicago, Philadelphia, and Boston). The peak total in 1926 was a little over 17 billion riders, while in 1940 the total was just over 13 billion riders. This was almost a 25 percent drop in total riders even though the population had grown by 13 percent. The loss in riders was entirely in the electric streetcar/trolley systems. They lost 7 billion riders (more than 50 percent), while the buses gained about 2.7 billion riders. Thus, although the buses gained nearly 140 percent, it wasn't enough to offset the electric streetcar/trolley loss.

In the decades after World War II, the number of rapid transit riders would hold relatively steady, around 2 billion, the buses would settle in at under 6 billion, and all others would trickle down to almost nothing on a comparable basis. The public transit system would consist mainly of buses and subways, at a total rider level of less than half that of 1926. More cities began to try subways and light rail systems near the end of the century, as will be discussed.

The big transition between the mid-1920s and 1940 was the rise of the bus at the expense of the electric streetcar/trolley. This was partly due to a basic problem of all public transit systems: they took on great debt to build competing systems while they were locked into contracts that did not permit them to raise fares. This is why nearly all public transit systems today are subsidized or owned by the municipalities they serve.

The untold story of this streetcar/trolley to bus transition is how General Motors and some unethical entrepreneurs undertook to buy up street-car/trolley lines and replace them with GM buses. Sometimes municipalities welcomed GM operatives with open arms, glad to get rid of the headaches of operating the lines but not realizing they would be replaced by GM buses.

The most famous — or notorious — name in this process is Roy Fitzgerald, who dropped out of school in 7th grade to go to work in a railroad construction camp. In 1916, Fitzgerald, newly married, took a night job in an automobile garage. This evolved into a job driving a bus taking miners to work, and when the owner of the bus retired, Fitzgerald and his brothers bought him out and began a long career in the bus business. By 1925, Fitzgerald and his four brothers were running 25 buses over a network of routes mainly in Minnesota. Soon they decided to challenge the interurban lines, which were essentially electrified streetcars running between cities, while the classical streetcar/trollies stuck to the intracities. It was not lost on the Fitzgeralds that road right-of-ways were free while the interurbans had to pay for theirs and also pay taxes to help build the roads. By 1933 the Fitzgeralds were running buses from Chicago to Paducah, Kentucky, 400 miles away.

General Motors, in the meantime, like all car manufacturers, was looking for ways to increase sales hurt by the Depression and the apparent saturation of the new car market. They had decided on the drastic step of trying to get intracity transit riders into cars and, at the least, buses. The two growth-hungry businesses, one huge, and one small and family owned (but profitable), essentially bumped into each other. Soon the Yellow Coach Company (a builder of buses controlled by GM) was financing the Fitzgeralds in attempts to buy out moribund municipal-owned (or power company–owned in cases where the power companies were taking over a big customer) trolley companies and replacing them with modern, comfortable buses. Fitzgerald would cut fares, then stand on the streets to see how many people were still walking to work, and then adjust fares as needed. Fitzgerald and GM was a marriage made in business heaven.

GM had tried earlier in the 1930s to convert cities from streetcars/trollies to buses, especially in New York City where it converted the world's largest streetcar network to buses in 18 months. But they preferred working in the background with Fitzgerald so that any angry straphangers would not take out their resentment on GM cars. Fitzgerald and GM took over nearly 100 transit systems and installed a bus monopoly in about 50 cities across the Midwest. Helped by the Wheeler-Reyburn Act of 1935, which forced many power company conglomerates to give up ownership of trolley systems, GM and Fitzgerald extended their operations to the West Coast.

By the time the 1940s arrived, the replacement of streetcars/trollies by buses was an established fact in much of the United States. Fitzgerald and friends were convicted in an anti-trust trial in 1949, but only received a slap on the wrist. It is hard to say if they did any real damage. The replacement of streetcars/trollies was an economic fact of life, and Fitzgerald and friends may have just accelerated an inevitable process.

January 30, 1942— The last Chevrolet to roll off the assembly line on this date bore the admonition of "the last Chevrolet off on January 30, 1942" written in chalk on the rear window. With the declaration of war after the attack on Pearl Harbor the previous month, car production was being shut down across the nation. The car companies would begin manufacturing trucks and tanks and planes for the war effort. Furthermore, all drivers would find their car trips limited by gasoline rationing.

The immediate problem relative to cars and driving was rubber. The Japanese conquests in the Far East had cut off the United States from 97 percent of its prewar rubber supply. What rubber could be had or manufactured synthetically was earmarked for the military. But civilians still depended on cars to get to work, and in a sense had to be saved from themselves in terms of nursing their car tires for the duration. On December 1, 1942, gasoline rationing began. A "nonessential" driver was given coupons and an "A" sticker to attach to the windshield. This permitted the driver four gallons of gas per week (later reduced to three). Car pool drivers and others could get an extra allotment and a "B" sticker. Important officials and doctors and the like rated a "C." The best sticker, an "X," permitted unlimited use. Congressmen immediately voted themselves X stickers.

As it turned out, about half the drivers in the United States were able to get either B or C stickers from their local rationing boards. Most drivers were able to get the gasoline they needed as truly unessential cars went up on blocks. More than 2.4 million cars were taken off the roads in 1943 and 1944, and car use fell to 60 percent of what it had been before the attack on Pearl Harbor. In a few areas, especially in the Northeast where German U-boat activity affected tanker deliveries, gasoline was simply unavailable. It was a common sight to see a line of cars trailing gasoline tankers on their delivery rounds. Drivers nursing their cars to last (and overseas GIs) were building a pent-up demand for new cars, and growing personal incomes would feed a great explosion of car buying after the war.

In the meantime the automotive industry was part of the "production miracle" that won the war for the United States and its allies. A famous example was Ford's new Willow Run (a suburb of Detroit) plant, heralded as a production masterpiece for B-24 "Liberator" bombers. After some initial problems that caused skeptics to call it the "Willit Run" plant, and after some West Coast aircraft executives sneered that the "blacksmiths" (car builders) would take a long time to learn to build a "watch" (airplanes), the plant leaped into production in the second half of 1943 and in 1944 was cranking out one new bomber each hour. They had a cost reduction factor of 40 percent. The blacksmiths had certainly learned, and the wartime output of B24 Liberator bombers totaled 8,685 planes. Stories of similar production success were common in the car building industry.

August 10, 1943 — Henry Ford II, the grandson of Henry Ford, arrived at the Ford River Rouge manufacturing facility after being recalled from the Navy to take over the company and its government contracts. Henry Ford II was one month short of his 26th birthday, and had never been involved in a serious way in the family business. He had been called back because of the problems at the Willow Run bomber plant (*see entry for* January 30, 1942), and with the rumors of Henry Ford's senility and dependence on a thug named Harry Bennett, government officials were concerned about the fulfillment of the contract. But the bomber production problems were solved almost as soon as Ford II arrived, and he went instead to the Rouge and concentrated, as he said later, mainly on "keeping his head down."

Henry Ford II blamed his own father's death on his grandfather, and the two had a strained relationship at best. The grandson attributed his father, Edsel Ford's, death to overwork and humiliation suffered at work, where Henry Ford ruled like an autocratic king. Henry Ford II pushed himself into the position of executive vice-president on April 10, 1944, and began to assume some real power. Finally, the mother of Henry Ford II, Eleanor Clay Ford, fearing the power of Harry Bennett, told Ford that if her son were not made president, she would sell her considerable amount of stock (about 40 percent of the company) and open the company to outsiders. She was supported by Clara Ford, Henry Ford's wife. On September 20, 1945, it was agreed that Henry Ford II would take over as president, and he immediately fired Harry Bennett. The Ford Motor Company was no longer the private fiefdom of Henry Ford and his whims. Ford died on April 7, 1947, just shy of his 84th birthday.

May 14, 1954 — Boeing unveiled its initial version of its highly secret B707 jet aircraft. Unable to interest anyone in the project, Boeing paid for the plane with its own money (a bargain at $16 million). The company gave the plane an internal designation of Model 367-80, and it soon became known among employees as the "dash-80." Once the plane was in action, the military ordered 29 units for use as a transport plane that could also serve as a refueling tanker. Ultimately, more than 800 planes would be built for the military.

Boeing then brought out the 707–120 version as a commercial passenger plane, and Pan American ordered six units and began coast-to-coast service in August 1958. In October of 1959 the 707–320 Intercontinental series began flying Pan American's New York-to-London route, and the course of commercial airline travel was changed forever. Within a few years all major airlines were flying jets.

The success of jet aircraft as a new mode of transportation can be measured by the number of intercity travelers choosing to fly rather than use the train. In 1950, airlines captured about 25 percent of all intercity distance travel. By 1960, as the use of jets was becoming widespread, airlines carried over 60 percent of intercity travel, and by the end of the 1960s, airlines carried 80 percent of intercity travel. In two decades, airline travel for this transportation segment increased by a factor greater than ten, while trains cut almost all their services by one-half. By the end of the 1960s, many trains had more crew (especially under outdated union rules) than they had passengers.

In a symbolic shift, the President of the United States no longer traveled by train, and the famed whistle-stop train tours by presidential candidates came to an end. The president used *Air Force One*, a modified Boeing 707, for his trips, and candidates made rushed campaign stops by jet as they traveled the country. Planes were in, trains were out. The railroads continued their trip towards irrelevance.

June 29, 1956— While in his hospital bed, where he was recovering from surgery, President Eisenhower signed the Federal Aid Highway Act of 1956. This innocuous-sounding piece of legislation was one of the most important acts of the federal government in the 20th century. The bill authorized $25 billion over the next twelve years to begin construction of a "National System of Interstate and Defense Highways." It also created a Highway Trust Fund that would receive income from taxes on gasoline and diesel fuel. An attractive part of the bill for the states was that it set the federal portion of highway construction at 90 percent, and the state portion at only 10 percent. In addition, there were considerations for advance acquisition of rights-of-way, and a number of standards for highway construction and route marking. It was intended that the interstate highway system be completed by 1972. It actually took until the end of the 20th century, and the costs went up accordingly. There was little complaint from the people because even though new costs were constantly being incurred, the roads were also being completed. The only sour note came later in the century, when people began to complain that the country was becoming clogged with highways.

The Highway Act was one of those rare pieces of legislation of which nearly everyone approved — at least initially. In 1956, 72 percent of American families owned an automobile. By 1970, the number would rise to 82 percent, with 28 percent of the families owning two or more automobiles. As a result, personal purchases of gasoline and automobiles more than doubled over the same period. The automobile was now a basic part of the lifestyle of almost every family, and the new interstate highways would allow people to move about as they wished, to an extent never before possible. As Tocqueville said of the Americans in his famous study in 1831, "once they migrate, they circulate."

A notable part of the lobbying for the new Highway Act was the so-called Yellow Book. This was actually just a pamphlet prepared by the Bureau of Public Roads, which was circulated among the members of Congress, and named after the color of its cover. It showed how the roughly 2,200 miles of interstate would be placed in the cities of each state. But it was a stroke of genius in that it was a thin pamphlet, with very little writing, that clearly showed the highways routes, using simple maps. This enabled congressmen to dramatically demonstrate to their constituents exactly what would result from their support of the act. The maps showed where the roads would go, and where the roads went construction funds and jobs would follow, and politicians at every level knew this.

The Highway Act had been defeated in 1954, because there were many controversies over how the road would be funded. In 1956, the Yellow Book went a long way towards creating support in Congress, especially after the funding argument was resolved. As a result, only one Representative whose city appeared in the Yellow Book voted against the 1956 Highway Act, and he failed to be reelected in 1956. At the end of the 20th century there some people claimed that a conspiracy had resulted in the government's embracing of highway transportation over other modes of transportation. If one were to label it a conspiracy, the involvement of almost every American would have to be recognized. Few acts were as popular in the nation as the Highway Act of 1956.

This act was probably the final death knell for railroads. As noted earlier (*see entry for* May 14, 1954), the switch to airplane travel for intercity trips was already seriously impacting railroads. As the new highways began to spread across the country, people began to drive longer distances, in addition to the shorter trips they were already making close to home. Drivers switching to personal cars for longer trips effectively meant the end of the railroads' significance as a means of transporting passengers.

Notably, the battle to get the Interstate Highway Act approved marked the end of the tenure of Thomas MacDonald. MacDonald had led the Bureau of Roads since 1919, and had been responsible for getting roads built in the United States for 35 years. MacDonald turned 70 in 1951, but he was able to continue past retirement age on a year-to-year basis, by appointment of the president. Eisenhower wanted his own men in the highway program, and on March 26, 1953, MacDonald was officially retired. Ironically, the king of roads went into retirement by taking the train to College Station, Texas, where he had been promised a job at Texas A&M College. He would not be involved in the biggest road-building program of them all.

The Interstate Highway Act proposed the construction of over 40,000 miles of roadway. The scope and difficulty of the undertaking was estimated to be comparable to constructing over 400 Pennsylvania Turnpikes, which at the time represented the state-of-the-art in road building. It was a massive project that would affect the entire nation. Less than two years into the program, the project grew from an initial estimate of $27 billion over 13 years to an estimate of $41 billion over 16 years, as a result of engineering changes and extensions. By 1976, 20 years after the program started, 38,000 miles of road had been opened at a cost of $62 billion dollars. Yet, even when the project was approaching completion, tax increases for the Highway Trust Fund would be required to maintain the new roads. National motel and fast-food chains clustered around the interstate highways, providing food and rest to car drivers and truckers, and local malls and shopping centers were built as close to an interstate exit as possible.

By design or by indifference, the nation had committed itself to transportation primarily by car and truck (during the 1950s the percentage of freight delivered by trucks on the interstate rose from one-sixth to one-quarter, an increase of roughly 50 percent). As the century progressed, controversies arose over pollution, overcrowded roadways and U.S. dependence on foreign oil, but for better or worse, in 1956 the American people had chosen the car — and accessible superhighways, which gave them the ability to travel when and where they wanted — as the key to their lifestyle.

1968—As a measure of how completely Americans had embraced the car culture, it was calculated in 1968 that one in six persons either made, sold, maintained, or drove motor vehicles for a living. There were 60,000 auto showrooms in the country, 211,000 service stations, and 114,000 automobile repair shops. Motels, mostly built close to highways, numbered 40,000. The process of motor vehicle construction consumed 20 percent of all steel and 60 percent of all rubber produced in the United States. The Asphalt Institute spoke of a "perpetual" cycle of new roads leading to more cars and gasoline usage (which fed new tax revenues into the Highway Trust Fund), which in turn led to new roads.

The rise of the automobile meant that, where there had been 20,000 passenger trains operating in the nation in 1928, 40 years later, in 1968, there were only 600 left. That was a reduction of roughly 97 percent. The famous Wabash Cannonball by 1968 ran from St. Louis to Detroit with only a baggage car, a coach, and a snack bar. Not surprisingly, railroads were trying to abandon passenger service and concentrate on freight. One surprising development in 1968 was the merger of long-time enemies the Pennsylvania Railroad and the New York Central Railroad. This was the strongest evidence yet that the railroads were in financial difficulties. The new railroad formed from the merger, the Penn Central, went into bankruptcy just two years later, in 1970.

January 22, 1970—The Boeing 747 began regularly scheduled service on this date on Pan American's New York–London route. It was the first so-called Jumbo Jet, but industry officials did not like the connotation with elephants and tried to introduce the term "Giant Jet." Workers in the industry soon coined the phrase "wide body" for the 747 and other planes that were developed to compete with it.

The 747 was the next big advance in commercial aviation when it was built. It could carry 500 passengers (350 is a more common load), but was so immense that it could be operated profitably with no passengers at all thanks to the capacity of its cargo bay. With a range of nearly 6,000 miles, it could theoretically cover a delivery range of halfway around the earth by flying either west or east from a given point.

In addition to the positive jolt it gave to commercial aviation, the massive 747 became famous for carrying the Space Shuttle piggyback when the shuttle landed in California and had to be transported back to its home base in Florida. In addition, although any plane carrying the president is named *Air Force One*, two modified 747s have each been designated a "flying White House." These planes are designed to carry everything the president needs to remain in control of the country from the air, and with a range of 9,600 miles, they can fly to nearly any place on earth nonstop from Washington, D.C. (halfway around the earth is roughly 12,500 miles).

May, 1971—The rail corporation known as Amtrak began operation. It was a result of the Rail Passenger Service Act of 1970, which gave railroads the right to carry only freight, allowing them to divest themselves of passenger service. The corporation was originally known as Railpax, but the name was considered a poor choice for several reasons. The official name was the National Rail Passenger Corporation, but Amtrak seemed a better choice for a popular designation: it was an easily remembered name that conveyed the sense of a national railroad organization.

Amtrak received $40 million in direct federal grants, and another $190 million from the participating railroads, payable in the form of locomotives and rolling stock if desired. Amtrak thus began operation with mostly used equipment, and maintained about half of the passenger train schedules that existed before it began. Amtrak has focused on the heavily traveled Boston–New York–Washington corridor, but it has never been able to pay its costs out of operating revenue.

By the end of the century Amtrak carried 22 million people yearly (75 million including contracted commuter services), and it would be the only long-distance train passenger service in the United States. But whether demand will ever grow enough to generate revenues high enough to make the corporation self-sustaining is an open question. Federal and state subsidies keep Amtrak alive, but just barely. Perhaps the biggest question is whether the country needs Amtrak-type train passenger services. Many people echo the sentiment expressed by Senator James Couzens in a Senate hearing in 1932, when he said: "Our railroads ... filled a great purpose, but if we had no railroads today, we never would think it necessary to build them." It must be noted that then–Senator Couzens was one of the original founders of the Ford Motor Company in 1903, and although he left the company in the mid-teens, his view may not have been completely objective. His opinion is still shared by many people, who see no need for a railroad-based general passenger service in the new century. Whether Amtrak will continue to survive by the skin of its teeth remains to be seen.

January, 1974— A law was passed remaking the Penn-Central Railroad, the result of a 1968 merger between the Pennsylvania Railroad and the New York Central Railroad that had gone bankrupt in 1970, into a new railroad called the Consolidated Rail Corporation or "Conrail." The new law also created the United States Railway Association (USRA) to improve railroad efficiency in certain areas before Conrail became formally incorporated in 1976. The USRA eliminated duplicate tracks and placed several bankrupt railroads within the Conrail system.

Congress granted the new railroad an incredible $2.1 billion for start-up costs, but in an ominous move, Conrail had to return to Congress for another $5 billion to keep the new operation alive. These grants could be likened to rearranging the deck chairs on the *Titanic*, but others saw it as partial compensation for the billions of dollars that the government had cost the railroads through overregulation and the imposition of ruinous labor laws during the 20th century.

October, 1980— President Jimmy Carter signed the Staggers Act. It was named after Representative Harley Staggers of West Virginia, although Jim Florio of New Jersey had introduced it into legislation. The Staggers Act eased regulation of the railroads. Congress was finally realizing the perilous condition of the railroads, especially with the new congressional pet project, Conrail (*see above entry*), requiring about a million dollars a day in subsidies. It helped that it was an election year, because Congress knew deregulation was generally popular with the public. Congress also knew that the public would not long tolerate such subsidies, because Conrail had been created based upon the supposition that it would become a profitable business.

The Staggers Act permitted railroads to cancel unprofitable services and routes, and to offer volume discounts to customers without the prior approval of the Interstate Commerce Commission (ICC). The railroads could also raise rates that fell below a certain percentage of costs. The ICC had oversight control of the rates, but it lost much of its regulatory power. Congress then tried to be evenhanded by passing a companion bill called the Motor Carrier Act (Senator Edward Kennedy, while challenging Carter for the Democratic Party's presidential nomination, had made motor deregulation a campaign theme). The Motor Carrier Act lifted some regulatory restrictions on truckers, allowing trucks and trains to compete for the nation's freight business without being unduly hampered by the ICC. The expectation was that prices would fall within the competitive atmosphere, while profits could still rise without the ICC's outdated and expensive restrictions.

The expectations were realized, especially by the railroads. In 1981 the industry had its most profitable year in a quarter-century, and Conrail struggled into profitability by 1985. The one aspect of regulation Congress did not attempt to undo were onerous labor laws, like the law requiring firemen to ride Amtrak trains pulled by diesels. Similarly, trains that could be operated by two people were required to carry five to seven employees, and all rail workers received a full day's pay whenever the train traveled over 100 miles, a legacy from the days when trains traveled much shorter distances. Rules of this sort would doom the trains to second-class competitive status, even after the ICC was phased out in 1995.

As a result, in the 1980s railroads cut costs and unprofitable track mileage until the unions realized that they had to overhaul labor agreements if they were going to keep any jobs at all. The new agreements cut the workforce by 60 percent, to two hundred thousand people. In return the railroads spent $3 billion to buy out workers' contracts. Coupled with new technology, this enabled the railroads to carry one-seventh more freight volume, with barely half as many freight cars and half the number of employees, by the mid-1980s.

The "container revolution" took place in the 1980s, in which items were packed in huge containers that were loaded directly from trains to trucks. Train companies began buying trucking companies, and vice-versa, or establishing working agreements, further blurring the lines between the two modes of transportation. The truckers and railroads tried to work together for a change, using the mode of transportation that was the most efficient for a given type of shipment. But eventually 78 percent of surface freight was carried by the astounding number of trucks on the nation's roads; over 42 million, operating for 220,000 trucking companies. Railroads have fought back with mega-mergers, recasting themselves as smaller regional railroads built on tracks bought from bankrupt lines or on tracks abandoned by the large railroads. These regional lines are more flexible than the big railroads, but the railroads in general have remained uncompetitive against the huge number of trucks battling for the same market.

The two businesses are still vastly different, and the basic route mileage of railroad tracks in the nation shrank by 48 percent between its peak in 1916 and the year 2000. No matter how optimistic one's view of the railroads, it must be admitted that they have lost the battle for the nation's freight hauling business to the trucking companies, and only Amtrak, wobbly as it is, carries on the passenger service battle. This is due to one fundamental difference between the two. Trains can go only where their tracks go, while trucks rely on roads, and thus can go almost anywhere. Even in the narrow area of commuter travel, only an extensive subway service like the one in New York, ten times bigger than any other, is as effective as the automobile in getting people close to their destination. Trains are becoming a vestige of the past.

September 29, 1986— Construction on the Metro Rail starter subway project in Los Angeles began. Home to more car drivers than any other urban areas, L.A. had finally decided to join other cities and build its own light rail/subway system. The agency in charge, the Southern California Rapid Transit District (RTD) had already bought a record 960 buses in 1982, but the agency still had to overcome reluctant taxpayers (who were hesitant to spend any money on mass transit) and irate bus riders (who thought all mass transit funds should be spent on buses). The controversy was typical of most mass transit projects.

The chief of the Los Angeles RTD, John A. Dyer, was an expert at getting mass transit funds from Washington, and the federal government produced more than $2.5 billion for the project. The RTD was eventually replaced by the Metropolitan Transit Authority, in 1994. Dyer left in 1988, long before the first section of the project opened in 1993.

The light rail/subway project in Los Angeles was part of a renewed nationwide interest in such projects. This renewed interest gained momentum in the 1970s, but the first step was actually taken in 1961 in the San Francisco Bay Area, when voters imposed a tax on themselves to construct a regional mass transit rail system. Within a decade, this vote resulted in the Bay Area Rapid Transit System, or BART. The new system consisted of rail lines in the East Bay and the West Bay, including a subway under part of San Francisco, connected by a four-and-a-half-mile tunnel under San Francisco Bay. BART made extensive use of automatic operation techniques.

In the meantime, in 1969, the Philadelphia Port Authority Transit Corporation, or PATCO, built a modernized extension of a previous shuttle line into New Jersey by way of the Delaware River Bridge, which connects Philadelphia and Camden, New Jersey. The light rail extension ran over an old railroad right-of-way to the bedroom community of Lindenwold, New Jersey, 12 miles from downtown Philadelphia.

BART and PATCO were built initially with local funds, but later drew on funds authorized originally in 1964 by the Urban Mass Transportation Act. Funding from this act also triggered the construction of rapid transit subway systems in Baltimore, Miami, Atlanta, and Washington, D.C. Thus, the 1970s and 1980s saw an expansion of traditional subway systems like the one in New York City, as well as light rail systems, in which congested downtown areas had subways and outlying areas had aboveground rail systems operating on separate rights-of-way.

The San Diego light rail system, opened in 1981, is held up as a model of the type of system that can be built with local funds, eschewing federal funds and the accompanying red tape. Similar systems have been built in Buffalo, Sacramento, San Jose, and Portland, Oregon. Regardless of how well these systems appear to operate, there are always critics who complain that the same thing could be accomplished with buses and subways at a fraction of the cost.

The United States Department of Transportation (DOT) has tried to alleviate the cost burden by providing grants that offer 75 percent federal funding and 25 percent local funding. Still, mass transit faced the same fundamental problem that had dogged it throughout the century: riders have never been willing to pay the fare levels required to make the systems profitable. Private companies were not anxious to get involved in a business where it was so hard to recoup costs, and over 90 percent of mass transit systems were publicly owned by the 1980s. This left local governments to undertake the long and tedious process of raising fares.

In spite of the optimism about the future of new subways and light rail systems, they have yet to make a notable impact on the nation's transportation systems in total. Even after nearly two decades of operation, the light rail portion of the Los Angeles Metrolink system carries about 34,000 riders a day, placing it far behind New York's Long Island Rail Road, which carries over 340,000 riders per day. The light rail systems in Chicago, Boston, and Philadelphia carry 287,000, 146,000, and 101,000 riders respectively. The Los Angeles system is estimated to carry only about one percent of the area's total commuters, and that doesn't take many cars off the freeways. But the Los Angeles system does exceed the ridership in San Francisco and Baltimore.

Light rail ridership remains insignificant when one considers the total number of commuters. In the gigantic New York system, New York mass transit ridership amounts to about 7 million riders a day, compared to the few hundred thousand carried by light rail in various other cities. New York towers over everyone else not only because it is the most populous city in the nation, but also because its subway system is one of the few that can take riders close to their downtown destinations as effectively as any other means of transportation. In Los Angeles, even if you add bus riders to the total, ridership is on the order of 1.5 million, far below New York, but far greater than light rail ridership alone.

The conclusion is that nearly everyone speaks favorably of light rail, but few people actually use it. There are even "class warfare" issues involved: bus riders, many of whom can't afford cars, complain that too much public money is spent on light rail services that primarily benefit the affluent, or at least those who can pay ticket prices of up to $300 dollars a month for the option of not driving to work. Light rail is a growing part of urban transportation, but it has yet to significantly impact traffic congestion in most cases.

Los Angeles is on the side of the angels in operating their Metro Transit Authority with its Metrolink train services, but the effort is largely symbolic. No one expects it to make a sizeable dent in the traffic flow in and around Los Angeles. The former executive director of the Los Angeles County Transportation Commission, Neil Patterson, a prime supporter of Metrolink, was quoted on January 7, 2003, in the Los Angeles *Times*, as saying that "the system we came up with was not meant to carry a gigantic portion of the area's commuters. We wanted to give people options, get some of those commuters out of their cars, expand the possibilities. And we wanted to get people to understand that rail could make a difference." A noble goal, but one that does not have a real impact on the area's traffic problems.

December 29, 1995— The Interstate Commerce Committee (ICC) was abolished by the ICC Termination Act of 1995. The ICC had existed almost 109 years, having been established in February of 1887. In a sense, 1995 marked the official end of the "Railroad era." The Staggers Act of 1980 pulled most of the teeth from the ICC's ability to regulate the railroads, and by 1995 the committee served no purpose because the railroads were no longer a viable transportation option. Railroads continued to develop new technologies and operating methods to maintain a niche in the freight business (roughly 25 percent), and Amtrak continued to try and establish itself in passenger operations and mass transit, but by the end of 1995 railroads were so insignificant as a mode of transportation that they were basically a thing of the past. The termination of the ICC essentially was an admission that regulating the railroads was like beating a very dead horse.

Some felt that the elimination of the ICC was a generation too late, while others insisted that it should have been eliminated a half-century ago, after World War II. The rise and fall of the ICC was a good demonstration of the problems associated with the regulation of industries in a free enterprise society. The federal government created the ICC in 1887, when trains had a true monopoly on transportation over all but short-distance travel. It took

20 years for the government to give the ICC the tools it needed to be effective in its regulatory role. The ICC's regulations and taxation did not begin to have any true effect on the railroads' behavior until after World War I, but by the 1920s and 1930s, only a few years after it had begun to accomplish anything, the railroads were no longer the monopoly the ICC had been created to fight.

However, the ICC continued its tough regulatory role against the railroads, while other modes of transportation, especially motor vehicles and airplanes, gained the upper hand. It didn't help the railroads that during the end of the 19th century and the beginning of the 20th century, they had behaved with terrible arrogance and actually lived up to the public's perception of them as robber barons. Thus, in spite of their outstanding performance during World War II, a move to eliminate — or ease the regulations of — the ICC would still have been met with fierce opposition.

Many experts feel that such a move would have been the only way to give the railroads a level playing field on which to compete with the other modes of transportation. The truth of the matter, whether that is true or whether it would have been favorable for the nation, can never be known. What is known is that the railroads faded from the picture after World War II, and by the end of the 20th century the only realistic options for transportation were motor vehicles (cars, trucks, and buses) and airplanes. Those choices require large expenditures for roads and road maintenance, and for the building and operation of airports. They also mean 135 million cars registered for operation in the nation, as well as 42 million trucks operating on the nation's four million miles of highways.

The 1990 census showed that of 115 million workers in the United States aged 16 or older, 99.8 million, or nearly 87 percent, got to work by car, motorcycle, or truck. Public transit of some sort was used by about 6 million, or 5 percent; about 5 million walked or rode a bike (a little over 4 percent); and the remaining 4.2 million (less than 4 percent) used other means or worked at home. Considering that about two-thirds of public transit is by bus, this means that over 90 percent of all workers nationwide commute via some sort of motor vehicle. If such things still count, more than 90 percent of anything certainly constitutes a monopoly, but it is a monopoly that nearly all Americans "conspire" to support. Clearly, in terms of public preference for commuting to work, the motor vehicle has far outpaced the competition.

The onerous regulations of the ICC notwithstanding, the demise of the railroads may have been inevitable. A flanged wheel on a rail is undoubtedly a very efficient way of moving almost anything. But it only can be moved where the rails go. Trains go from depot to depot or spur line to spur line. Trucks can run from door to door, and highways are literally everywhere for the convenient operation of both cars and trucks. Anyone who has ever seen a motorist circling in a mall parking lot to get a space a few steps closer to an entrance knows that a typical driver wants to drive directly to his or her destination. This limitation above may have doomed trains as a mode of public transportation in spite of any other considerations. Present-day railroads depend on high-technology diesel locomotives, and are greatly affected by the price and availability of oil and fuel. Our present dependence on motor vehicles and airplanes may have been inevitable from any point of view.

September 11, 2001 — In a horrific attack that will have many long-lasting consequences, the twin towers of the World Trade Center in New York were destroyed, and the Pentagon was damaged by terrorists using hijacked airplanes as weapons. A fourth hijacked airliner crashed in the hills of western Pennsylvania after a rebellion by its doomed passengers caused the plane to fall short of its intended target — possibly the White House. About 3,000 people were killed in the attacks.

One effect of the attacks was the devastation of the airline industry. People hesitated to fly because of the hijackings, and the security measures instituted to guard against further hijackings produced long lines and hours of delay at all airports. For some months parking and traffic restrictions made it difficult to even reach airports and pick up or deliver passengers. Passenger loads fell, and this was especially hard on the larger airlines with relatively high labor costs. Two of the biggest airlines in the country, American Airlines (first in size) and United Airlines (third), had such severe problems they had to consider filing for bankruptcy. United would eventually seek bankruptcy protection, while American Airlines just avoided doing so at the last moment. Both airlines are working to achieve new labor efficiencies and return to profitability. Hawaiian Airlines, which depended almost totally on tourist traffic between Los Angeles and Hawaii, simply declared bankruptcy and closed its doors. Air Canada, based in Canada but very active in the United States, also went into bankruptcy.

This is a good example of how an unexpected disaster can affect an entire industry. Whether and when the airline industry will return to its previous level cannot be predicted. It seems certain that an effective airline transportation system will continue to exist in the United States, but some companies may not be able to adjust and survive. Those that do will have to learn methods of operation that substantially reduce costs and permit profits to be made on fewer total industry passengers. Southwest Airlines has succeeded with a "no frills" approach, and may be one model for the future.

April 17, 2002 — The American Public Transportation Association (APTA) stated in a news release that the number of Americans using public transportation increased in 2001 for the sixth straight year. Total ridership in 2001 was 9.5 billion, the highest in the nation since 1960. If one excludes the old-time trolleys, and the "forced" public ridership during and just after World War II, a case could be made that ridership on public transit was at an all-time high in 2001. But even excluding the special-case years of World War II, total mass transit ridership was nearly twice as high in 1926. On a per-capita basis, it was nearly five times as high.

The key point is more Americans are using mass transit than at any time in the past 40 years, and the number increases a little more every year. As noted before, over 90 percent of people still travel to work using motor vehicles (including a small percentage on buses), but there is a slow and steady increase in the use of mass transit. Of course, the increase would have to continue for many more decades to have a significant impact on transportation overall.

December 14, 2002—An article in the *Los Angeles Times* described how the automobile industry was "pulling the plug" on the all-electric car. This issue had been of special interest in California over the past decade, and any car-related issue in California is of interest to the whole nation. More cars are sold in California than in any other state, and California alone has permission from the federal government to have more stringent pollution standards than federal requirements. The story of California and the electric car is discussed in detail in another volume in this series, *The Chronology of Energy*, published by McFarland & Company in 2003.

California had decided it would force drivers into electric cars by raising the state emission standards to a level that officials thought could be met only by electric cars. However, car manufacturers have a massive investment to protect in the internal combustion engine (ICE). Some Japanese car manufacturers were able to develop technology that permitted the low-emission standard to be met even with the ICE. In addition, Japanese manufacturers began to offer "hybrid" cars, which combine a small ICE *and* an engine that operates electrically. This hybrid solved the problem of most electric cars, in that they have very poor acceleration and they need to be recharged often. In addition, standard electric cars use very large batteries that can make the car unstable. In the hybrid model, the ICE provides standard driving performance while at the same time charging a conventional battery. The battery provides power sufficient to operate in the electrical mode, and it is regularly charged by the ICE. Some cars alternate between electrical and ICE operation; other cars keep both on all the time, applying a particular mode as required by driving conditions. The relatively small ICE gets very good mileage and produces low emissions, while the electrical operation produces no pollution at all.

Hybrid cars quickly became popular, and automobile manufacturers consider them the wave of the future, at least until the fuel cell car can be fully developed. Accordingly, they discontinued their fully electric vehicles, seeing no market for them. California, to some extent, was left with egg on its face: its Air Resources Board was sure manufacturers would have to build electric cars to meet the standards, and the board expected to have fleets of electric cars now operating in California. They even arranged to have parking lots built with outlets to recharge electric cars. The outlets are still there; but there are no electric cars to use them.

This demonstrates the difficulty of trying to force drivers to change their behavior. When seatbelts were first introduced in the United States, there was no question that they would save lives, but there was a lot of resistance to laws mandating their use. Drivers would agree that seatbelts save lives, but they didn't want to be forced to use them. Eventually seatbelts became a standard part of people's lives, and most drivers now buckle up automatically.

It has frequently been commented upon that people's attachment to their cars and their driving habits is deeply rooted in psychology. The old saying "a man's home is his castle" could easily be stated as "a man's car is his castle." In his book *The Automobile Business Since 1945* (1971), Lawrence J. White observed that "a car perhaps represents one of the last bastions of privacy in modern America, where a man is away from his family and his boss and colleagues. He can sing, shout, scratch his ears, turn the radio on loud, and make threatening gestures and shout obscenities at other motorists, all without fear of social rebuke." The same thing could be said of all drivers, regardless of gender.

This kind of freedom seems natural to Americans, but it is also desired by people around the world. Ford Motor Company once did a study showing that as soon as a nation's gross national product passed a certain level, the population began buying cars immediately. The allure of personal transportation — and the freedom of choices it allows — seems only human. It may be stronger in America than in other places, because Americans consider personal freedom and "the pursuit of happiness" to be almost their birthright.

This helps explain why the state of California was unable to force people into electric cars. Drivers did not want, and did not like, electric cars. They found them to be unacceptably underpowered, and a problem to recharge frequently. When one talks about solving traffic problems, this psychological resistance must be taken into account, or the solution will never produce the results expected. Despite the periodic revival of different kinds of mass transit, the fact remains that over 90 percent of people who travel to work do so in some kind of motor vehicle. A significant number of people who use mass transit do so because they cannot afford to own an automobile, or the percentage would probably be higher. Everybody wants relief from traffic congestion, but Americans are unwilling to change their driving patterns or give up their cars to achieve the goal. Automated freeways and other high-technology solutions to traffic problems have practically no chance of being adopted in America, because drivers simply will not give up control of their vehicle. America's love affair with the automobile results in almost 50,000 driving-related deaths a year, but it is a price the country had so far been willing to pay.

December 24, 2002— The General Motors Corporation (GM) began an end-of-the-year advertising blitz about their new hybrid cars and fuel-cell cars. On this date, they ran a full-page ad in the *Los Angeles Times* describing their fuel-cell vehicle (the HydroGen3), built for Federal Express to use for deliveries in downtown Tokyo, Japan. This would be a difficult test for any car, especially one using fuel-cell technology. The advertisement was intended to run nationwide, and made the point that if the car could perform well in Tokyo, it certainly could perform well in midtown Manhattan in New York City, or on a "cruise down the 405," the famous freeway in Los Angeles. General Motors stated in the advertisement that fuel cells "may well be the future power source for just about everything." The ad also pointed out that there is "no more difficult application of fuel cell technology than the automobile. If we can crack it, we can change the world."

The fuel cell car is presently the Holy Grail of automobile manufacturers. Its operation and applications are described in detail in the companion volume in this series, *The Chronology of Energy* (McFarland). Fuel cells operate by an electrochemical process that is the reverse of batteries. If oxygen and hydrogen are constantly supplied to a fuel cell, it will constantly produce electricity and water vapor. The fuel cell is like a battery that never runs down, as long as the basic ingredients of oxygen and hydrogen are supplied. It is comparable to an internal combustion motor that will run forever, as long as fuel is supplied. The hope is for a fuel cell-powered electric car that can provide much better performance than can currently be achieved by battery-powered electric cars. There would also be a considerable market for stationery fuel cells, to give companies and homeowners a constant supply of electricity in the event of problems with the central power system. This is an attractive prospect in areas that often lose power due to storms. Fuel cells are also very attractive to the military, because long-lasting self-contained sources of power would be very valuable for use in military vehicles.

On December 27, 2002, an article in the *Los Angeles Times* described General Motors' plans to produce at least one million hybrid vehicles by 2007. General Motors was also talking to the Pentagon about building tens of thousands more hybrid vehicles for military use. Thus, in just three days,

General Motors made its mark in the two newest motor vehicle technologies: fuel cells and hybrids. Cars powered with fuel cells ideally would utilize hydrogen as a fuel rather than gasoline, greatly reducing America's need for imported oil (some interim designs would use methanol to create the hydrogen). The discussions between General Motors and the Department of Defense are especially notable, because historically the Department of Defense has paid for the development of many technologies that eventually appeared in consumer products. If successful, these two efforts by General Motors would go a long way towards creating the so-called hydrogen economy that is the dream of many environmentalists.

About a week later, on January 5, 2003, General Motors announced, at the Detroit Automobile Show, that they were planning to produce hybrid sport utility vehicles (SUVs). The very profitable SUV has become a bestseller in the automotive market, but they have generally been considered unsuited to hybrid operation because they are large and powerful. But GM is confident that they can include SUVs in the one million hybrid cars they expect to produce by 2007, as they had announced on December 27, 2002.

If GM can even come close to this forecast, they will challenge Japanese carmakers Toyota and Honda for leadership in the hybrid car market. GM also said that after federal and state tax incentives are applied, they believe their hybrid car models will not cost much more than traditional cars powered by internal combustion engines. This is very important, because although many people are in favor of hybrid cars, they don't want to pay more than they would for a conventional car. An important advantage of the hybrid car is that it has lower emission than conventional cars, and this will be very important in meeting California's stringent air quality regulations. Since California, as noted before, is the largest car-buying state in the nation, meeting their requirements is obviously very important to car manufacturers.

Thad Malesh, director of the Alternate Power Technology Practice at J.D. Power and Associates, stated, "GM is clearly responding to the early lead that the Asians have held." But GM says its timing is just right. According to Larry Burns, GM's Vice President of Research, Development, and Planning, "None of these new technologies mattered if they don't sell in high volumes." As of 2003 Toyota and Honda were selling about 20,000 each of their hybrid cars annually, a volume Burns considered only enough to fill a tiny niche market.

So-called mild hybrids use a gasoline engine, with electric motors for auxiliary power and to restart the gasoline engines, which shut down when the vehicle stops. Bigger "full" hybrids also use the electric drive to provide extra power when climbing hills or passing other vehicles. GM will be the first American carmaker to use the mild hybrid, in several of its 2004 models. According to Burns, mild hybrids will improve fuel economy by about

12 percent, but, with a special engine management system, they can increase the fuel savings by as much as 20 percent by shutting down half the cylinders at highway speeds on V8 and V6 engines.

Other car manufacturers plan to sell SUV hybrids in 2005 and 2006, or later, but by then GM plans to have launched a full hybrid model featuring a dual electric motor system designed to improve the mileage of SUVs by 50 percent, to about 40 miles per gallon. With all of these plans underway, the hybrid car's widespread appearance in the market no longer seems a question of "if" but of "when." For decades the hydrogen economy has been just over the horizon, but never here. With fuel cell cars promised to be a major part of the automobile market by 2010, the hydrogen economy may actually become a reality. But, as discussed in *The Chronology of Energy*, the goal of a hydrogen economy has always seemed just within reach, yet has continually eluded our grasp. It remains to be seen whether the goal will be achieved in the first decades of the 21st century.

February 16, 2003—An article in the *Los Angeles Times* questions whether the Ford Motor Company will be able to survive more than a few more years. Ford made a big comeback after World War II with the advertising slogan "There's a Ford in your future"; the title of the article in the *Times* was "But Is There a Future in Ford?" Ford's problems seemed especially poignant because 2003 marked the 100th anniversary of Henry Ford's founding of the Ford Motor Company (*see entry for* June 16, 1903).

The article stated that Ford lost more than $5 billion in 2002, and that some industry consultants questioned whether Ford chairman William Clay "Bill" Ford, Jr., (great-grandson of Henry Ford and a nephew of Henry Ford II) had the necessary experience and "smarts" to turn the company around. Henry Ford II, the grandson of Henry Ford, had been called back from naval duty to rescue the company as World War II wound down, but the competitive environment for car manufacturers has changed drastically since that time.

Bill Ford has said in several speeches that "we have come back from adversity many times before, and we're going to do it again." Ford's stated aim is to earn $7 billion in pretax profits by 2007. Some consultants don't think Ford will survive beyond 2008, at least as an independent company. The key problem is that automobile makers today have to look at their business as a global one, and worldwide there is a manufacturing capacity of about 55 million cars a year, but a customer base of only about 32 million. There are potentially many new customers in Asia, Eastern Europe, and Latin America, but these markets have yet to be fully developed, and doing so will not be cheap.

Any company hoping to increase sales needs new products that are truly eye-catching. "If companies can't develop new products, they are doomed" says J. Ferron, senior analyst at PriceWaterhouseCooper's, an automotive consulting practice based in Detroit. Today those new products must include hybrid and fuel cell–based cars. The Ford Motor Company currently has about $26 billion in cash and liquid assets, so it has the money to bring out the new products it needs, but it has to plan carefully.

One quietly whispered thought is that Ford could merge or form some sort of working agreement with its archrival, General Motors. Although certain to raise antitrust issues, such an arrangement would give the United States a major player in the world automotive market. To bring new hybrid and fuel cell–powered cars to market is a very expensive process. Companies that are not in this product market may not survive. Just in the United States, several hundred car companies have disappeared since the beginning of the century, including about a half-dozen since World War II, among them names like Hudson, Nash, Packard and Studebaker. With an independent Chrysler disappearing into Daimler-Chrysler, there are only two major American car manufacturers left — Ford and General Motors. A merger or working agreement between them would create a single huge company in the United States, but with the Japanese and Daimler-Chrysler manufacturing cars here as well, and with all manufacturers in the world aiming at the United States as a prime automotive market, the word "monopoly" would not have the same sting in the automotive business as in other areas. An American company choosing to manufacture television sets in the U.S. would have a monopoly in terms of being the only United States company doing so, but it would not have a monopoly in terms of market share, and would have to compete with all the foreign manufacturers also selling televisions in the U.S. In a global economy, "monopoly" doesn't mean what it used to.

Considered objectively, automotive manufacturers have done a good job bringing technology to bear on the marketplace. Cars are ten times cleaner now in terms of emissions as they were 40 years ago. Pollution has been greatly reduced in the nation's cities, especially with the removal of lead from gasoline. Cars in general are much more fuel-efficient than they were 30 years ago. Perhaps most importantly, the research done by car manufacturers has brought us much closer to a hydrogen economy — and freedom from imported oil — than ever.

This progress has come partly through more stringent regulations, but also through the fact that few manufacturers are as market-sensitive as car manufacturers. Market forces can be more effective than governmental pressure in bringing positive change, as California's edict meant to bring electric cars into widespread use demonstrated. Clearly the personal automobile (and trucks and buses) and the highway system in the United States have swept away all other modes of transportation. Perhaps a huge corporation like the one that would emerge from Ford–GM merger or working agreement is the best way for American car companies to address the gigantic — and highly competitive — global automobile market.

March 6, 2003 — It was announced in New York City that bus, subway, and commuter train fares would jump by 50 cents, to a total of $2.00, effective May 4, 2003. This would be the first fare increase since November of 1995. Opponents of the increase immediately went to court to find a judge who would block the move. The judge first refused, but a few weeks later, on Wednesday, May 14, he ruled the fare increase should be reversed because the agency in charge had deliberately misrepresented its financial condition. The agency immediately said it would appeal. In the meantime the agency pointed out that rolling back the new fares, which had started on May 4 as scheduled, would create a "logistical nightmare" requiring "12,000 pieces of equipment, including the city's 4,500 buses" to be retrofitted. The cost of this retrofit would be over $2 million.

The episode is just one in a long line of examples of how difficult it is to operate a mass transit system and why private companies want no part of it. In essence, no matter how many hairs are split on arcane issues of bookkeeping, The Metropolitan Transportation Authority (MTA) is a non-profit operation, and is simply trying to recover in fares a percentage of the cost of operating the system. Fares often pay only 40 or 50 percent of a mass transit system's costs. But riders of publicly operated mass transit systems anywhere in the country (and publicly operated systems are essentially the only kind left) always complain when they are asked to pay fares that reflect the non-subsidized costs of operating the system. Mass transit systems are expensive to operate, in part because they were developed at a time when labor costs — which now typically make up 80 percent of a system's budget — were very low. As long as municipalities continue to operate mass transit systems, battles with the public over fare increases will probably take place. Present subsidies for mass transit systems provide from 45 percent to 70 percent of operating costs, which means that riders pay only 30 to 55 percent, but any attempt to increase fares is still met with howls of protest.

The proposed increase to $2.00 in New York would bring them even with Philadelphia, which only recently increased its basic cash fare for subways to $2.00. Fares are $1.75 in Atlanta, $1.50 in Chicago, $1.25 in San Francisco, and $1.00 in Boston. The old-time standard fare of a nickel or dime is long gone, but the fare wars go on.

April 14, 2003 — British Airways and Air France jointly announced that they would discontinue the supersonic Concorde's commercial service in October 2003. The Concorde had been in service for 27 years, and in spite of fares that reached $13,000 round-trip between New York and London, was never a great commercial success. The Concorde primarily survived as an ego boost for Great Britain and France, but the ever-changing demands of the airline market made the Concorde too impractical to operate, even as a symbol of aircraft prowess.

The customer base for the Concorde consisted of celebrities and rich executives who were willing to pay high prices to cut the time needed to fly across the Atlantic nearly in half— to three hours. Those same customers have turned to private jets that can operate out of small airports on their own schedule, in the process avoiding all the common airport hassles, including security guards and the ever-curious public. If travel time is measured door-to-door, private jets are competitive with the Concorde, in spite of its much greater flight speed. The Concorde also lacked the cachet of owning one's own personal jet.

Ordinary citizens have long ignored things like the Concorde in favor of cheaper fares and more flexible travel schedules. Travel consultant David Newkirk, quoted in the *Los Angeles Times* on this date, said "private flying is what first class used to be, and first and business class is where the old coach used to be, and coach is replacing the old greyhound bus." On one hand, movie star John Travolta flies his own Boeing 707, while on the other hand even business travelers flock to "no-frills" airlines like Southwest. "The market is splitting between extremes," says Richard Aboulafia, an aviation expert with the consulting firm Teal Group. As a result, Boeing Corporation recently dropped plans to build a super-fast passenger plane called the Sonic Cruiser. For its customers, speed was out and the ability to carry lots of passengers efficiently on many routes was in (the cramped Concorde could only carry about 100 passengers comfortably). The United States government came to a similar conclusion in the late 1960s and declined to get into the supersonic game. The Concorde was initially opposed by environmentalists because of engine noise, sonic booms, and the fact that they regularly flew at 50,000 feet, at least 10,000 feet higher than conventional airplanes, and there were fears it would damage the fragile atmosphere at that altitude.

The beginning of the end for the Concorde came in 1994 when it stopped service to Dulles Airport in Washington, D.C., due to declining demand. Many thought a crash caused by runway debris at Charles de Gaulle Airport in Paris that killed 113 people would be the end for the Concorde, but after keeping it grounded for more than a year, British Airways and Air France decided to resume operating the fleet (five planes in France and seven in England). Nonetheless the end was near, and the official announcement came on this date. There were plans to give the fleet to museums after the planes made their final flights, but the founder of Virgin Atlantic Airways, Ltd., Richard Branson, has expressed interest in taking the planes from British Airways and keeping them in service.

The Concorde is a good example of an idea that never made sense on a commercial basis, but that its sponsoring governments were determined to have anyway. The transportation business is very market-driven, and it is a wonder that the Concorde lasted as long as it did. It could serve as a lesson to groups that push hard for electrical cars for environmental reasons, but won't accept the fact that nobody wants to drive them. The market is responding to hybrid and fuel cell cars, and most experts think that the trend will continue, and grow.

Chronology Summary

The history of transportation in the United States is a dramatic one. From the founding of the colonies, through the Revolutionary War in 1776, and on into the 19th century, modes of transportation differed little from those found in most of the civilized world for the past 2000 years: floating in various conveyances on water; traveling on foot; riding on the backs of animals; and riding in wheeled carts or wagons that were pulled by animals (or people) on roads of varying quality. But about 50 years after the Revolution, the train made its appearance in the United States. It was an historic moment, and transportation changed forever.

The train swept all other modes of transportation before it, and from about 1830 to the end of the 19th century it was the primary means of transportation, especially over longer distances. But as trains gained complete monopoly status, the owners of railroads abused their power and angered citizens and governments. The governments struck back in the early 20th century, and curtailed the power of railroads by regulation and taxation. At nearly the same time, especially from 1908 onward, motor vehicles and airplanes, driven by the internal combustion engine, became practical alternatives to trains.

The rest of the 20th century was an ongoing story of new developments in motor vehicles and airplanes, and the slow death of trains, due to competition in the marketplace and strangulation by government regulations intensely applied long past the time they were needed. By the end of the 20th century, motor vehicles and airplanes had relegated railroads to obscurity, largely a vestige of the past, and billions of dollars had been spent by the government to build highways and airports.

At the beginning of the 21st century, airlines were severely affected by the horrific terrorist attack on September 11, 2001, and a number of airlines were struggling to stay alive. Transportation by motor vehicle was by far the preferred method in the United States, whether it be goods by truck, commuters by bus, or general transportation by private car. Car manufacturers worldwide were developing cars that could run in hybrid (gas and electric) modes or be powered by fuel cells. These techniques were meant to reduce pollution from car emissions, while reducing the country's dependence on imported oil to produce gasoline.

The development of these new processes was moving at a reasonable pace, and initial results were promising. Nothing on the horizon appeared capable of replacing the private car, or buses and trucks, in their applications. For the foreseeable future, in the United States and around the world, transportation would continue to be dominated by those modes that depended on motor vehicles.

APPENDIX 1:
CARS REGISTERED
in the United States

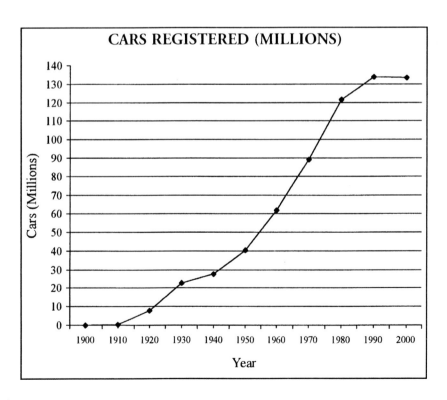

CARS REGISTERED (MILLIONS)

Year	Cars (Millions)
2000	133.5
1990	133.7
1980	121.6
1970	89.2
1960	61.7
1950	40.5
1940	27.5
1930	23.0
1920	8.1
1910	0.5
1900	0.008

The graph in Appendix 1 shows cars registered in the United States from 1900 to 2000. In 1900, there were only 8,000 cars registered in the United States and the car business was just beginning. By 1910, the number of registrations had jumped to 458,377. That was the beginning of the infiltration of automobiles into the fabric of the nation. By 1920, the number of registrations exceeded 8 million, and it grew toward 100 million from that point.

As can be seen from the plot, there was a slight slowing of the number of registrations after 1930, the result of the Depression in the 1930s and the discontinuation of automobile manufacturing during World War II. However, the pent-up demand for automobiles caused an explosion in car registrations after 1950. By 1960, there were over 61 million cars registered in the United States, more than double the number registered in 1940. In 1975, the number of registered cars crossed 100 million for the first time.

There were a total of 133.6 million cars registered in the United States in 2000. This number is actually slightly below the number of registered cars in 1990. This indicates that there are so many cars now in use in the United States that the number scrapped every year is approaching the number of new sales every year. In that sense, the market could be viewed as saturated. Even if new car sales did nothing more than replace the number scrapped each year, the United States would still be the top automotive market in the world. Cars are ubiquitous in the United States, a fact that doesn't seem likely to change in the near future.

Appendix 2:
Railroad Mileage
in the United States

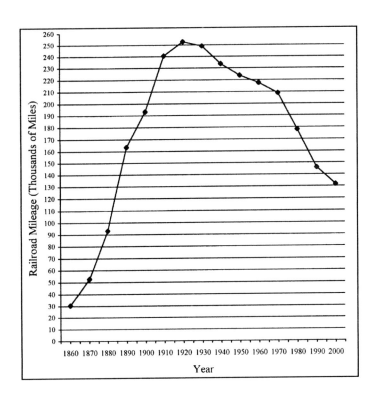

Year	Mileage (thousands)
1860	30.6
1870	52.9
1880	93.3
1890	163.6
1900	193.3
1910	240.4
1920	252.8
1930	249.0
1940	233.7
1950	223.8
1960	217.6
1970	205.8
1980	178.1
1990	146.0
2000	131.8

The graph in Appendix 2 shows the growth of railroad mileage in the United States between 1860 and the year 2000. This mileage is from point to point in the United States, and does not include more than one track between points. At the peak of the railroad business, multiple tracks were common. The plot therefore shows the growth of the railroads in terms of their penetration into different parts of the nation, and not necessarily in terms of the number of tracks that were finally laid in very highly traveled areas (such as between New York City and Chicago).

The plot shows that by 1860 railroad mileage in the United States was over 30,000 miles, even though railroads had only begun in 1830. By 1870, after the transcontinental railroad was opened, there were nearly 53,000 miles of track in the United States. The track mileage in the United States has consistently been the highest in the world ever since trains started operation in the beginning of the 19th century.

Railroad track mileage in the United States peaked in 1916, at 254,036 miles. By then, the Interstate Commerce Commission (ICC) was beginning to have a real effect, through regulation and taxation, on the railroad industry. Prior to then, since its creation in 1887, the ICC had been treated as a joke by the railroad barons. Woodrow Wilson was also reelected to the presidency in 1916, and he would take over the railroads in 1917 due to their infuriating behavior in World War I. In almost every way, 1916 marked the apex of the railroads in the United States. From 1916 onward, railroads steadily fell out of favor with the United States Congress. New track mileage was still being built, but from 1966 forward the number of miles abandoned exceeded the new mileage built.

Appendix 3:
Trolley and Bus Patronage

in the United States

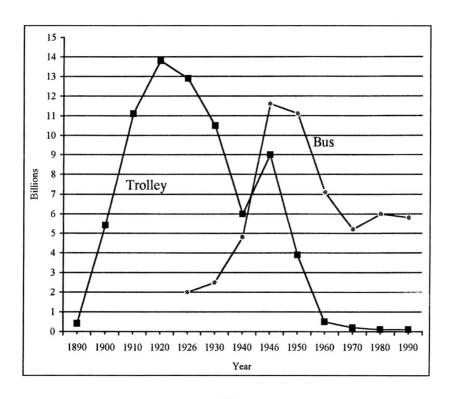

Patronage (in Billions)

Year	Trolley	Bus
1890	0.41	
1900	5.4	
1910	11.1	
1920	13.8	
1926	12.9	2.0
1930	10.5	2.5
1940	6.0	4.8
1946	9.0	11.6
1950	3.9	11.1
1960	0.5	7.1
1970	0.2	5.2
1980	0.1	6.0
1990	0.1	5.8

The graph in Appendix 3 shows the total patronage in terms of billions of riders per year, for trolleys and buses, between 1890 and 1990. The peak for trolleys, reached in 1920, is far above the peak for buses, which was reached in 1946. The year 1926 (see Appendix 4) was the peak year for total transit riders of all types in the history of the United States. The use of trolleys was already in decline by then, and their patronage continued to decline as General Motors and some other entrepreneurs bought up bankrupt trolley lines and replaced them with GM buses.

The replacement of the trolleys with buses violated a number of antitrust rules, as described in the text of the chronology. However, when trials were finally held in the late 1940s, the defendants only received a figurative slap on the wrist. It is not clear that the actions of General Motors and their conspirators did more than accelerate an already inevitable trend in terms of the demise of the trolleys.

The trolleys suffered from the key problem of all mass transit systems, i.e., the trolley operators had to agree not to substantially increase fares over the life of the franchise. Since labor accounts for about 80 percent of the total costs of operating a mass transit system, the labor cost increases of the 1920s and especially the 1930s caused most trolley systems to go bankrupt, as they could not recover the increased labor costs with increased fares. The only trolley systems that survived were those that were operated as a municipal service. It was very easy for General Motors and it associates to take over the bankrupt trolley systems and replace them with buses, because most municipalities were glad to be rid of the trolley systems. Today, the municipalities subsidize around 50 to 70 percent of the cost of their mass transit systems, and the prime vehicle used for mass transit is now the bus. The replacement of trolleys with buses was probably inevitable, regardless of behind-the-scenes maneuvering by General Motors.

Buses started in 1926 with a patronage level of nearly two billion. The patronage rose sharply from there as trolleys disappeared. The peak use of buses occurred in 1946, when continuing restrictions on automobile usage and manufacture drove people to use mass transit, including soldiers returning from World War II. Bus usage has declined since that date, as the use of mass transit has also declined. Bus patrons today make up about two-thirds of total mass transit riders. In that sense, even mass transit is primarily dependent on motor vehicles.

APPENDIX 4:
TOTAL MASS
TRANSIT PATRONAGE
in the United States

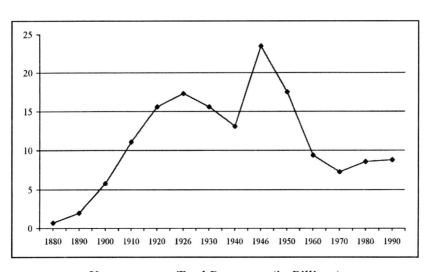

Year	Total Patronage (in Billions)
1880	0.7
1890	2.0
1900	5.8

Year	Total Patronage (in Billions)
1910	11.1
1920	15.6
1926	17.3
1930	15.6
1940	13.1
1946	23.5
1950	17.5
1960	9.4
1970	7.3
1980	8.6
1990	8.8

The graph in Appendix 4 shows the total patronage of mass transit between the years 1880 and 1990. Total mass transit includes all riders on trolleys, buses, subways, light rail, and elevated trains (such as in New York and Chicago). Total patronage reached an interim peak in 1926, when 17.3 billion people utilized the various forms of mass transit. Patronage declined after 1926, but in the 1940s, World War II restrictions were imposed on automobile usage and manufacture. As a result, in 1946, a new all-time high was reached in the utilization of mass transit. But ridership quickly declined, as the war ended and people returned to their first preference, private automobiles.

Total mass transit ridership is currently just below 10 billion people, with two-thirds of patronage provided by bus riders. Subways primarily account for the remainder. Much has been made of recent increases in the use of light rail and similar systems, but they only account for a drop in the bucket in terms of total mass transit patronage. For example, New York, which has by far the most utilized light rail system, counts only a few hundred thousand light rail riders per day, while the entire New York system carries in its total system patronage of over 7 million riders per day. Light rail therefore accounts for at less than five percent of the total.

Over 90 percent of all workers commute to work in some sort of motor vehicle. Mass transit would be even less of a factor in transportation if not for the fact that most municipalities subsidize at least half of the cost of operating a mass transit system. In Los Angeles, about 70 percent of the cost of mass transit systems is subsidized by the city. In spite of this, municipalities face widespread public resistance to any increase in fares.

The median income of bus riders is about $12,000 a year, while the average user of light rail makes about $22,000 per year. In theory, the average bus rider cannot really afford to pay much for bus transportation, nor can they afford to buy and operate a car. So the major cities subsidize mass transit, mainly in the form of buses. This activity is perceived as providing an important service to low-income persons, who otherwise would have great difficulty in moving about the city. Mass transit will never be self-supporting, but the operation of such systems is viewed as a public service, providing public transportation to low-income people, and providing jobs to bus drivers and related personnel.

Appendix 5:
Mass Transit Trips
per Capita

in the United States

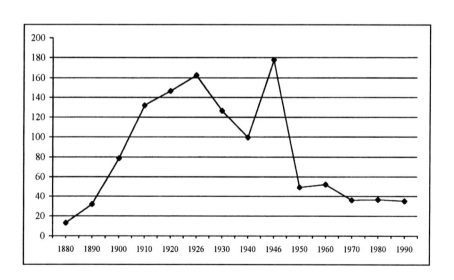

Year	Per Capita
1880	13.1
1890	32.1

Year	Per Capita
1900	78.8
1910	132.0
1920	146.8
1926	162.7
1930	126.7
1940	99.4
1946	177.7
1950	49.5
1960	52.6
1970	36.1
1980	36.6
1990	35.2

The graph in Appendix 5 shows the per capita use of mass transit in the United States. This graph clearly shows that mass transit use is now essentially stagnant. From 1880 to about 1920, mass transit grew in almost direct proportion to the population. The per capita use of mass transit went up as the population went up, and thus the total use grew sharply, as shown in Appendix 4. After the mid–1920s, the per capita use of mass transit started declining sharply, as more and more people were driving personal automobiles.

In 1946, the per capita use reached an all-time high, as World War II restrictions on car usage and manufacture forced people to use mass transit. As soon as car manufacturing resumed and restrictions were lifted, people began ignoring mass transit in favor of the personal automobile. By 1990, the per capita use of mass transit in terms of trips per year per person was down to the mid 30s, the same place it had been in 1890. This means essentially that in the 100 years between 1890 and 1990, the number of mass transit trips taken by the average person had not increased at all.

Essentially, this says that there is a fixed core percentage of the population that uses mass transit. This core group expanded from the late 1880s until 1926, and then began to decline. The special circumstances of World War II brought a new peak in 1946, but then the core group shrank back to a roughly fixed size between 1950 and the present time. No matter how the average population increases, only from about 35 to 53 mass transit trips per person have been taken in the United States in the last forty-some years.

The small increases noted in the six years between 1996 and 2001 (*see entry for* April 17, 2002) are basically a result of the small increases in the total population in the same period. Mass transit usage will probably continue to increase in the future, as long as the population of the United States also increases. Otherwise, one cannot escape the fact that only about five percent of the commuters in the United States utilize mass transit.

BIBLIOGRAPHY

This bibliography shows the key books consulted in putting together this chronology. Probably the most broadly useful book in the bibliography is *Ford: The Times, the Man, the Company*, by Allan Nevins and Frank Ernest Hill. Allan Nevins is a professional historian, and his book is especially useful in describing the times in which Henry Ford helped form the Ford Motor Company and propeled it to the top of the automotive world. The description of the background against which Ford accomplished his task is extremely useful in understanding that critical period in the history of transportation in the United States.

In the same way, Fred Howard's *Wilbur and Orville: A Biography of the Wright Brothers* also captures the times and climate in which the Wright brothers worked, carefully describing the beginning of the worldwide airplane business in the process.

A third interesting and informative book, about the development and construction of the transcontinental railroad, is *Nothing Like It in the World*, by Stephen E. Ambrose. Ambrose describes in great detail the building of the transcontinental railroad and the men, from laborers to railroad company presidents, who made it happen. Besides relating an incredible adventure in American history, this book also provides a wealth of historical data about the transcontinental railroad (and railroads in general) in the United States.

Another useful and readable book is *Trains Across the Continent*, by Rudolph Daniels. It is a textbook about railroads in the United States and Canada from the early 1800s to the present, and Daniels is obviously very passionate about railroads and greatly mourns their demise. It probably has more information about railroads than you really want to know, but there are few pertinent items about the development of railroads in the United States that are not in this book.

Finally, I want to highly recommend *The American Heritage History of the Automobile in America*, which was published by American Heritage under the direction of Stephen Sears. It includes a great deal of material about the beginning of the automobile business in America. The details about the early days of the industry and the men who built the major companies in the industry were a valuable asset in researching and writing this book.

Ambrose, Stephen E. *Nothing Like It in the World*. New York: Touchstone, 2000.

Automobile Quarterly. *The American Car Since 1775*. New York: Automobile Quarterly, 1971.

Berkebile, Don H., ed. *American Carriages, Sleighs, Sulkies, and Carts*. New York: Dover Publications, 1977.

_____. *Horse-Drawn Commercial Vehicles*. New York: Dover Publications, 1989.

Bridgewater, William, and Seymour Kurtz, Editors. *The Columbia Encyclopedia*, 3rd ed. New York: Columbia University Press, 1963.

Caper, William. *100 Ships and Planes that Changed World History*. San Mateo, CA: Bluewood Books, 2002.

Chant, Christopher and John Batchelor. *A Century of Triumph: The History of Aviation*. New York: Free Press, 2002.

Cudahy, Brian J. *Cash, Tokens, and Transfers: A History of Urban Mass Transit in North America*. New York: Fordham University Press, 1990.

Daniels, Rudolph. *Trains Across the Continent*. Bloomington: Indiana University Press, 1997.

Goddard, Stephen B. *Getting There: The Epic Struggle Between Road and Rail in the American Century*. Chicago: University of Chicago Press, 1994.

Hood, Clifton. *722 Miles: The Building of the Subways and How They Transformed New York*. Baltimore: Johns Hopkins University Press, 1993.

Howard, Fred. *Wilbur and Orville: A Biography of the Wright Brothers*. New York: Ballantine Books, 1987.

Jakab, Peter L. *Visions of a Flying Machine: The Wright Brothers and the Process of Invention*. Washington: Smithsonian Institution Press, 1990.

Kane, Joseph Nathan. *The Kane Book of Famous First Facts and Records in the United States*. New York: Ace Books, 1974.

Lacey, Robert. *Ford: The Men and the Machine*. Boston: Little, Brown, 1986.

Lewis, Tom. *Divided Highways: Building the Interstate Highways, Transforming American Life*. New York: Viking Penguin, 1997.

Madsen, Axel. *The Deal Maker: How William C. Durant Made General Motors*. New York: J. Wiley & Sons, 1999.

McCullough, David. *John Adams*. New York: Simon and Schuster, 2001.

McGeveran, William A., Jr., Editorial Director. *The World Almanac and Book of Facts: 2003*. New York: World Almanac Books, 2003.

Meyer, Stephen, III. *The Five Dollar Day: Labor Management and Social Control in the Ford Motor Company, 1908-1921*. Albany: State University of New York Press, Albany, 1981.

Nevins, Allan, and Frank Ernest Hill. *Ford: The Times, the Man, the Company.* New York: Charles Scribner's Sons, 1954.

Sears, Stephen W. *The American Heritage History of the Automobile in America.* New York: American Heritage Publishing Co., 1977.

Shulman, Seth. *Unlocking the Sky: Glenn Hammond Curtiss and the Race to Invent the Airplane.* New York: HarperCollins, 2002.

Taub, Eric. *Taurus: The Making of the Car That Saved Ford.* New York: Dutton, 1991.

Tiner, John Hudson. *100 Scientists Who Shaped World History.* San Mateo, CA: Bluewood Books, 2000.

Weisberger, Bernard A. *The Dream Maker: William C. Durant, Founder of General Motors.* Boston: Little, Brown, 1979.

Weitzman, David. *Model T: How Henry Ford Built a Legend.* New York: Crown Publishers, 2002.

Yenne, Bill. *100 Inventions That Shaped World History.* San Mateo, CA: Bluewood Books, 1993.

INDEX